The Gospel of 2012
According to Ayahuasca

The end of faith and the beginning of knowingness

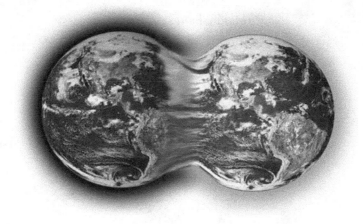

by Greg Caton

~~ Final 2013 Edition ~~

Text Copyright © 2012-2013 by Greg Caton

Design Copyright © 2012 Santuario del Corazón, Inc.

Cover Design by: Jack Bracewell

Published in the United States by
Santuario del Corazón, Inc.
8345 NW 66th Street #7093
Miami, Florida 33166

Print ISBN: 978-0-939955-09-1
e-Book ISBN: 978-0-939955-03-9

Library of Congress Catalog Number: 2012908758

Book Website
www.Gospel2012.com
Email: contact@Gospel2012.com

Give feedback on the book at:
feedback@Gospel2012.com

Printed on Demand

Book cover photo (Galatic Core) image taken by
NASA's Jet Propulsion Laboratory.

"Still, honor Me in this.
Everything unfolds in due time.
Don't be so anxious that you have to open up
your Christmas gift before Christmas.
Just respect the unfoldment,
because it's all part of the Plan."

~ Source from *The Gospel of 2012 According to Ayahuasca*

Acknowledgements

I want to thank my wife, Cathryn, for her support and encouragement. Given everything we have endured in our twenty year sojourn together, I can honestly say she is the epitome of the persevering, long-suffering spouse. During our darkest hours in dealing with dark forces, her belief in what we were doing and commitment to our cosmic mission never wavered.

Author's Preface: 2013

The monograph before you is the result of a series of "ayahuasca vision quests" taken from November, 2011 to May, 2012. It recounts a series of astonishing revelations that were received, which, taken together, constitute the most deeply spiritual experiences of my life. The channelled content focuses on events that were set to occur at "the end of 2012," roughly corresponding to what has been variously described as the "2012 phenomenon." The copy you are reading is the second and final version.

In the grossest sense, **The Gospel of 2012** was a abject failure. Not only did the majority of events described never happen, but the public never responded to the book itself. The number of books sold and freebie digital editions that were downloaded from the book's website (gospel2012. com) never exceeded five thousand copies -- paltry compared to the 45,000 copies my first book sold. This is attributable to the timing of the publication -- mere months prior to the Passage described in the book -- and commitments on my part that prevented an aggressive marketing effort.

After the first of the year (2013), I began to receive correspondence asking about my "take" on 2012 and why so many people were received similar messages that, like the prophecies of ages past, "failed to materialize." At the same time, friends who were on their own spiritual quest and felt that something momentous was set to occur at the end of their year, shared their bewilderment.

I have taken more than 125 ayahuasca vision quests to date, and there is no question that the fabric of time is quite elastic in the realms which from knowledge of possible future time lines can be viewed. Could it be that the events that were seen with such clarity when experienced have been delayed? Are they glimpses of a reality that has emerged on a parallel universe, and not throughout the "multiverse"? Are the manifestations described symbolic of a deeper set of phenomena that should not be interpreted literally? Was "Gospel" the presentation of an optimal outcome to world events, if only our own belief in our power to co-create were fully functioning? Or is possible that "The Gospel of 2012" represents a homogenous "what if" scenario that was pieced together from data within my own subconscious?

No doubt these are all good questions, albeit beyond the scope of this Preface to compose a thorough analysis, let alone one that would be satisfying to most readers. In retrospect, I will say this in my own defense: the realism, consistency, congruity, even originality of the material I was "presented" was and is unmistakeable. It was beyond anything I could have created in the most creative moments of my everyday, normal state of consciousness. Moreover, on numerous occasions I was given material that is not in keeping with my own beliefs, opinions, and in some cases, even my background or experience. Even my wife, Cathryn, commented several times that I appeared to be in touch with something much greater, more loving, authoritative, and awe-inspiring than myself. This was clearly something "other than me."

The intensity of the experiences I describe in this book rivaled other events I have been shown which did come to pass, sometimes with shocking accuracy. Perhaps this should come as no surprise, since no clairvoyant (and I'm using that term broadly here) is accurate 100% of the time.

Then again, perhaps this is the nature of prophecy. It resists precision and reliability, demanding that we seek out our own Truth – a theme that runs throughout this book. If I were to tell you that I – or any other person with a gift for peering into the future – were clearly seeing events that would not happen for another 2,000 years, not until after the year 4,000 A.D., you would probably think that odd. Nonetheless, this is an article of faith for hundreds of millons of Christians around the world who believe that the visions of St. John of Patmos as they appear in the Book of Revelations are a roadmap for predicting world affairs, nearly two thousand years after they were written.

With this in mind, the issue of relevancy becomes pertinent. Is there a value in reading entheogenic "divine revelations" if these do not occur within a period that is clearly specified within the revelations themselves?

Maybe that is the ultimate value of "Gospel of 2012." That each of us should envision an outcome for "our" universe that befits our most endearing and cherished beliefs. For my part, I cannot imagine a more glorious ending than the one you are about to read.

Greg Caton
Cuenca, Ecuador
February 4, 2013

Glossary

Akashic Records

The akashic records are described as containing all knowledge of human experience and the history of the cosmos. They are metaphorically described as a library; other analogies commonly found in discourse on the subject include a "universal supercomputer" and the "Mind of God."

Archetype

An archetype (Pronounced: ahr"-ki-tahyp) is a universally understood symbol, term,or pattern of behavior, a prototype upon which others are copied, patterned, or emulated. Archetypes are often used in myths and storytelling across different cultures.

In psychology, an archetype is a model of a person, personality, or behavior.

In philosophy, archetypes have, since Plato, referred to ideal forms of the perceived or sensible objects or types.

In the analysis of personality, the term archetype is often broadly used to refer to:

- In Jungian psychology a collectively inherited unconscious idea, pattern of thought, image, etc., universally present in individual psyches. It is in the *Jungian sense that the word archetype* is used throughout the book.

- The original pattern or model from which all things of the same kind   are copied or on which they are based; a model or first form; prototype.

Ayahuasca

Ayahuasca (Pronounced: a'-ya-was"-ka) is any of various psychoactive infusions or decoctions prepared from the Banisteriopsis spp. vine, and usually mixed with the leaves of dimethyltryptamine (DMT)-containing species of shrubs from the Psychotria genus.

Ayahuasca is used largely as a religious sacrament. When used for its medicinal purposes ayahuasca affects the human consciousness for less than six hours beginning half an hour after consumption, and peaking after two hours. The remedy also has cardiovascular effects, moderately increasing both heart rate and diastolic blood pressure.

The psychedelic effects of ayahuasca include visual and auditory stimulation, the mixing of sensory modalities, and psychological introspection that may lead to great elation, fear, or illumination. Its purgative properties are important (known as la purga or "the purge"). The intense vomiting and occasional diarrhea it induces can clear the body of worms. See (http://en.wikipedia.org/wiki/Ayahuasca.)

There are a wide variety of ayahuasca brews that can be obtained in the Western Amazon. Botanical sources for the DMT vary some, and the strength and recommended dosage for the finished brew itself vary even more widely. "Ayahuasca negra" refers to one particular brew well known to ayahuaqueros in the central, Ecuadorean Amazon. It is very concentrated compared to most other finished ayahuasca preparations – the average dose being no more than 30 ml. It is called "negra" because of the type of ayahuasca vine used and to denote high concentration. The finished preparation, like nearly all ayahuasca brews, is still a shade of dark orange.

Ayahuasquero

A shaman who specializes in the preparation, use, range of experiences, and local ceremonial practices related to ayahuasca entheogenic compounds.

Bhagavad Gita

The Bhagavad Gita (pronounced: bahg'-uh-vahd-gee"-tah): also referred to as *Gita*, is a 700-verse Hindu scripture that is part of the ancient Sanskrit epic, Mahabharata. However, those branches of Hinduism that give it the status of an Upanishad also consider it a Sruti or "revealed text." As it is taken to represent a summary of the Upanishadic teachings, it is also called "the Upanishad of the Upanishads."

Black Swan Event

The *black swan theory or theory of black swan events* is a metaphor that encapsulates the concept that an 'event' is a surprise (to the observer) and has a major impact. After the fact, the event is rationalized by hindsight.

The theory was developed by Nassim Nicholas Taleb to explain:

- The disproportionate role of high-impact, hard-to-predict, and rare events that are beyond the realm of normal expectations in history, science, finance and technology

- The non-computability of the probability of the consequential rare events using scientific methods (owing to the very nature of small probabilities)

- The psychological biases that make people individually and collectively blind to uncertainty and unaware of the massive role of the rare event in historical affairs

Clairaudience/Claircognizance

In the field of parapsychology, clairaudience (from late 17th century French clair 'clear' and audience 'hearing') is a form of extra-sensory perception wherein a person acquires information by paranormal auditory means. Claircognizance is often considered to be a form of clairvoyance involving a knowingness of future events devoid of visual spectacle. — Wikipedia (https://en.wikipedia.org/wiki/Clairaudience#Cl airaudience_.28hearing.2Flistening.29).

Emanuel Swedenborg

Emanuel Swedenborg was a Swedish scientist, philosopher, theologian and Christian mystic. He termed himself a "Servant of the Lord Jesus Christ" in *True Christian Religion*. In fact, this was the title of one of his works

Swedenborg had a prolific career as an inventor and scientist. In 1741, at the age of fifty-three, he entered into a spiritual phase in which he eventually began to experience dreams and visions beginning on Easter weekend April 6, 1744. This culminated in a spiritual awakening, whereupon he claimed he was appointed by the Lord to write a heavenly doctrine to reform Christianity. He claimed that the Lord had opened his spiritual eyes, so that from then on he could freely visit heaven and hell, and talk with angels, demons and other spirits.

Entheogens

An entheogen, meaning "generating the divine within," is a psychoactive substance used in a religious, shamanic, or spiritual context. The term entheogen is used to refer to any psychoactive substances when used for their religious or spiritual effects,

- Datura — Datura belongs to the classic "witches' weeds," along with deadly nightshade, henbane, and mandrake. Most parts of the plants contain toxic hallucinogens, and datura has a long history of use for causing delirious states and death. It was well known as an essential ingredient of love potions and witches' brews. Wikipedia: (http://

en.wikipedia.org/wiki/Datura)

- Peyote — Author's Note: I've never taken peyote, but I have friends who have used it extensively. One friend from Texas who I met while in prison tells me that peyote is his entheogen of choice. "The experience is clean, pure, and nearly every journey has brought me spiritual knowledge that has made the quest worthwhile. There is a reason it was so central to the spiritual lives of indigenous peoples of the U.S. Southwest." Wikipedia (http://en.wikipedia.org/wiki/Peyote)

- Psilocybin Mushrooms — Author's Note: My personal experience with psilocybin mushrooms is limited to what I experienced while living in Louisiana. Every "spiritual traveler" has their preferences, and for spiritual exploration, I found mushrooms to be an inferior tool — for whatever reason. The goal of entheogenic use is not to "get high," and, in fact, in the higher spiritual realms, using entheogens for anything less than one's personal spiritual growth is highly frowned upon. In my own case I found psilocybin mushrooms more hallucinatory than revelatory, so I discontinued use. Wikipedia (http://en.wikipedia.org/wiki/Psilocybin_mushrooms).

- San Pedro (Echinopsis pachanoi) — Author's Note: I only journeyed with San Pedro once — in a location not far from Cuenca. Again, all travelers have a preference as to their mode of transportation. I found the experience — for me personally — to be inferior to ayahuasca. Wikipedia (http://en.wikipedia.org/wiki/Echinopsis_pachanoi).

- Ibogaine — I haven't taken this African entheogen, but I know people who have. I mention it here because it appears to be increasingly more popular. Ibogaine is a naturally occurring psychoactive substance found in a number of plants, principally in a member of the Apocynaceae family known as Iboga (Tabernanthe iboga). A hallucinogen with both psychedelic and dissociative properties, the substance is banned in some countries; in other countries, it is being used to treat addiction to opiates, methamphetamine and other drugs. Derivatives of ibogaine that lack the substance's hallucinogenic properties are under development. Wikipedia (http://en.wikipedia.org/wiki/Ibogaine) .

Gospel

(As meant in the title of this book)

Gospel: pronounced [gos-puhl] — noun

> 1. A doctrine maintained to be of great importance

Meditopia®

A free online book detailing the author's experiences as an herbalist. Read it for free at www.meditopia.org.

Meme

A meme is "an idea, behavior or style that spreads from person to person within a culture."A meme acts as a unit for carrying cultural ideas, symbols or practices, which can be transmitted from one mind to another through writing, speech, gestures, rituals or other imitable phenomena.

Psychonaut

Psychonaut refers to a spiritual seeker who uses one or more entheogens (such as ayahuasca) as an adjunct to their psychic travels.

Shaman

Shaman is a person who acts as intermediary between the natural and supernatural worlds, using magic to cure illness, foretell the future, control spiritual forces, etc. (Pronounced: shah"-muhn).

Transhumanistic

Transhumanism is an international intellectual and cultural movement that affirms the possibility and desirability of fundamentally transforming the human condition by developing and making widely available technologies to eliminate aging and to greatly enhance human intellectual, physical, and psychological capacities.Transhumanist thinkers study the potential benefits and dangers of emerging technologies that could overcome fundamental human limitations, as well as study the ethical matters involved in developing and using such technologies. They predict that human beings may eventually be able to transform themselves into beings with such greatly expanded abilities as to merit the label "post-human."

The text of Gospel 2012 takes a decidedly negative position as it relates to this line of thinking, as it subverts the natural process of spiritual evolution and serves as a tool of co-optation by dark forces.

As so many of the propositions of high technology, the promise and the practice are at odds.

Table of Contents

Book One
The Message

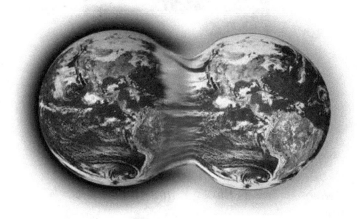

"Our heart is the key because our true self is within our heart. Whereas our physical body is only a temporary 'shell' — flesh and blood that will one day turn into dust — our relationship with our True Source, our connection to the Love, is eternal."

~ Irmansyah Effendi: *Smile to Your Heart Meditations* (book)

"There is a light that shines beyond all things on Earth, beyond us all, beyond the very highest heavens. This is the light that shines in our heart."

~ Chandogya Upanishad 3.13.7

Introduction:

My Initiation Into Ayahuasca & Clairaudience

"Crazy Mom and Industrial Dad."

My brother, Daniel, coined this expression when we were teenagers to describe the seemingly dysfunctional relationship between our parents. Although teenagers aren't always known to appreciate their parents or give them proper respect, this pejorative was made humorous by its strange underpinnings.

Myron, our father, was a workaholic — both during his managerial day job and in the unending serial projects he would nurse into the late night hours. He had no enduring hobbies, didn't appear to enjoy leisure as much as other fathers did, and in all of my years growing up, I never once recall him sitting down to read a book to completion — a simple pleasure I have enjoyed my entire adult life.

By contrast, our mother, Jeannine, was, well — I'm not sure where to begin. Imagine a middle-aged woman who spends the majority of her waking hours sitting on a couch or bed, starring into the heavens while in an ever-present state of altered consciousness, speaking to unseen spiritual entities . . . *often aloud* . . . undeterred by the presence of her husband, children, and sometimes even neighbors and friends.

Few would view my brother's impish remark as unfounded; after all, a good many people would call that crazy. And yet my brother and I, irrespective of an occasional stab at humor didn't view our mother's off-planet preoccupations with the same misgivings as outsiders did. Even our father, who in moments of frustration would refer to his mystic wife as "that doggone Hungarian," appeared to show respect for her abilities. It is often said that there is a fine line between the remarkably gifted and the psychologically broken — between the "asane" and the insane, and in this instance, our mother's remarkable gifts were as difficult to discount as were her socially unacceptable, inexplicable, and too-often embarrassing behavior.

Not that he didn't harbor doubts. On a couple occasions in our late-teens and early twenties, Myron had our mother placed in the care of psychiatrists for testing to confirm what seemed all too obvious. Each time the diagnosis was the same — "she's perfectly normal." And to hear our father tell the story, the psychiatrists would usually needle him with questions afterwards, as if to say, "Maybe you're the one who's crazy . . . for dragging your wife in here and wasting our time!" This unintended result always startled our father. But Jeannine was never surprised.

Our father, to his credit, was as forbearing and generous as any spouse could possibly be given the situation. In fact, although our parents permanently separated in 1978, he never stopped caring for Jeannine. Despite leaving to fulfill a natural desire to have a real-world relationship within a dimension with which he was familiar, he continued to support her for the rest of her physical life. When our mother died in 2005, she had not worked full-time since the mid-1950's, and it could be said that her cloistered spiritual journeys were financially supported for her last twenty-seven years of monastic living. Few separated husbands would be so accommodating.

One of the unexpected gifts that resulted from Jeannine's spiritual sojourns was clairvoyance[1], an ability she possessed until infirmity became a regular companion during her last few years. I could write a separate book just citing numerous examples, but one of the most memorable concerned an event that occurred as I was passing into adulthood.

During my last year of high school, my mother happened to tell me that I was going to join the Navy and travel overseas, and that I'd be actively involved for *three years.* Even in those days my anti-establishment views on a variety of positions were not entirely unknown to my parents. And so I am sure she must have anticipated that I would take issue with her prediction.

"There's no way I would ever JOIN the military!" I countered most emphatically. "Not the Navy, the Army . . . it doesn't matter what branch. What, are you kidding, after all that nonsense in Vietnam? You may have been right in seeing a lot of other future events, but you're wrong this time."

---

1   Clairvoyance — The term clairvoyance (from French clair meaning "clear" and voyance meaning   "vision") is used to refer to the ability to gain information about an object, person, location or physical event through means other than the known human senses, a form of extra-sensory perception. A person said to have the ability of clairvoyance is referred to as a clairvoyant ("one who sees clearly").

Less than two years later, in the summer of 1975, I graduated from junior college. Mentally exhausted from taking too many classes, feeling the effects of a serious recession where I had problems finding a job, I contemplated the unthinkable. A friend told me about a program that was being offered by the U.S. Navy at the time. I thought about it for several weeks while I continued my fruitless effort to find gainful employment, and then I threw in the towel and enlisted. The contract called for a six year term with *three years of active duty*.

My brother and I have spoken at length over the years about the many extraordinary experiences we had with our mother while growing up. Strangely, it is often in connection with premonitions of our own which manifested precisely as we foresaw them. At such times, it has become almost unavoidable to contemplate where such abilities came from. And yet, my brother and I have never had a problem acknowledging that our talents paled in comparison to our mother's.

In 2006 my wife, Cathryn, and I began making trips to Ecuador, in preparation for our family's move to that country the following year. During my false imprisonment in the U.S., an event I detail at considerable length elsewhere, I happened to develop friendships with several inmates who had experimented extensively with "entheogens."[2] Most people, *the unwashed uninitiated*, associate natural botanicals and other similar life forms, such as datura, peyote, psilocybin mushrooms, San Pedro, ibogaine, and ayahuasca *(see glossary for entheogen details)* — most of which I have now used in my psychic explorations — with recreational drug use. This facet of the "common narrative" is (especially in the U.S.) undoubtedly connected with governmental attempts to demonize tools of accessing higher consciousness, which they cannot control. The simple truth is that most regular users of these materials use them for strictly spiritual purposes.

On the night of August 25, 2006, I took my first ayahuasca journey in a small retreat on Ecuador's Pacific Coast. During this four hour session, I experienced a profound awareness of other inter-dimensional realms. In the months that followed Cathryn would journey with me, only to decide one day in 2008 that she had had enough. Experiencing little more than the sight of strange shapes and patterns and a propensity to vomit profusely, she found no spiritual value in our vision questing. "I guess it's really true what the ayahuasqueros (see glossary) say," she

---

2   Entheogens — Wikipedia: (http://en.wikipedia.org/wiki/Entheogen)

told me, "You don't choose ayahuasca . . . ayahuasca chooses you."

It soon became apparent to me that with the aid of ayahuasca, I was able to do many things that my mother could do without the use of entheogens. The exception was that my journeys tended towards "clairaudience" and "claircognizance." It wasn't so much that I saw the future, as I heard it or attained a sudden knowingness of it.

In the early morning hours of November 11, 2006, I experienced the first of what would become a series of contacts with the ayahuasca plant spirit. These telepathic communications, as real as any verbal communication you might have in your ordinary waking state, only intensified with time. This led to communications with other plant spirits and then to other higher intelligences. Soon thereafter, I learned how to "navigate" through different dimensions, realms, and etheric planes. I began to identify my surroundings and the beings in my presence by their vibration. In doing so I could determine an entity's intentions — primarily to determine if they were malevolent — at which point I could choose to communicate with them or "travel" somewhere else. My experiences became less passive and more proactive. To someone who has never communicated with higher intelligences, with or without the aid of entheogens, such claims may sound fantastic, if not fictitious — a by-product of taking hallucinogens in the first place. However to someone who is familiar with inter-dimensional territory, it is our everyday world of waking consciousness that appears fabricated and unreal.

Our "multiverse" is filled with countless marvels that defy the common narrative and accentuate the narrow-mindedness of our educational systems. To have travelled where I have been is to understand that there is no star, planet, moon, asteroid, comet — indeed, no mass in the vast reaches of the heavens, which is not teeming with life. We fail to recognize this because we pollute the organs of our perception and aristo-centrically limit our definition of what we call life.

One of the downsides to my explorations is the realization that we live on a planet that is suffering from a severe cycle of engineered devolution. Words cannot express the places I have been where there are societies of intelligent beings living in a state of unspeakable bliss and harmony, unencumbered by the pathological systems of exploitation, greed, and control that currently grip our own global community. It has made my returns to my ordinary state of consciousness depressing.

Sometime in 2009 my vision quests began to take a distinct change in direction. They became less visual, more abstract, and the focus of the subject matter of the intelligences I chose to communicate with turned to events on my own planet. I did not consciously choose this change; it happened on its own. These journeys were interrupted by my illegal kidnapping, an event orchestrated by the U.S. Government which I foresaw in a vision quest eleven days before it happened. (I devote considerable space to this politically-charged event in my online book *Meditopia®*.) [3]

In September, 2011, I returned to my family in Ecuador and continued where I had left off.

Sometime in November, 2011, I began to get the first of what would become an extensive series of communications concerning events that would begin at the "end of 2012." This book is an attempt to put these telepathic messages into an organic tapestry that is organized, coherent, chronological, easy to read and understand, yet remain true and faithful to the content of the original messages and the intent of the intelligence who communicated them.

Because this book is being published in the middle of 2012, following a cavalcade of publications and internet materials that have come out over the past 15 years concerning the significance of the year 2012, (particularly the time after the winter solstice on December 21), the reader might naturally ask, "Why yet another book about 2012?"

Everyone who reads this book needs to know that I have taken great care to relegate my own position to little more than messenger, transcriber, and organizer. Yes, there is considerable material to be found elsewhere concerning entheogenic explorations, indigenous prophecies, psychic channeling, remote viewing, and even government investigations into the "2012 phenomenon." However, what separates my own communications from anything I have found elsewhere is the sheer volume and detail of the messages themselves. There is a coherence and logic to what you will read here that I have found nowhere else. If this were not true, I would have felt most disinclined to issue yet *another 2012 book*, especially at this date.

The next logical question after examining this manuscript is, "Could any of this be true?" In other words, "What are the chances that events will unfold exactly as this text describes?" In posing this query, one may assume that because I am the conduit for the release of this

---

3   See *Meditopia®* -- The scandal that resulted from my illegal kidnapping in 2009 is covered in Chapter 3, Section 3 of that online work: (http:// www.meditopia.org/chap3-3. htm)

information, I must automatically be its staunchest proponent. I am not. In fact, I am not embarrassed to say that despite an unmistakable "air of Divine authority" that emanates from most of the text, no one has struggled harder with this question than I have. Even a "psychic traveler" as influential as Emanuel Swedenborg[4] was careful to note that one must be cautious when practicing the craft — for there are all manner of malignant, tale-weaving, parasitic entities, just as we have on earth, which you will encounter within the countless planes that human consciousness is capable of exploring.

A reader's assumption that I hold the position of principal proponent is bolstered by the simple observation that the vast majority of those who claim to "channel" information, from beings clearly "not of this world," assume a supportive role. The messages themselves become woven into the fabric of their ego. They speak as if whatever they are passing along must be infallible, despite the fact that the historical record is brimming with supposed "divine messages" with specific prophetic pronouncements that subsequently failed to materialize. The source of my own skepticism is best explained in an experience that happened to me only five years ago.

In early 2007 I happened to read <u>Mass Dreams of the Future</u>, a book detailing the work of Dr. Helen Wambach and Dr. Chet Snow.[5] Their research was primarily conducted in the 1980's. This remarkable book dutifully recounts amazingly synchronous future events given by a variety of patients who were hypnotized and subjected to "future life progressions." After years of conducting "past life regressions" for therapeutic purposes, Dr. Waumbach decided to use the same techniques to unearth what her patients saw in their future life.

What did these people see? Around the turn of the century, they collectively saw cataclysmic events that mimic the prophecies of Edgar Cayce: global nuclear war, massive loss of life, huge earth changes and acceleration in our engineered devolution that parallels the gravest fictional accounts one may find in twentieth century dystopian literature.

In May, 2007, Cathryn and I travelled to Sedona, Arizona to attend a "wisdom gathering" of indigenous speakers who discussed what their traditions foresaw in future events. Speakers at this conference included actor and native activist, Russell Means,[6] speaking for the Lakota tribe,

---

4   See glossary.
5   Mass Dreams of the Future — See (www.chetsnow.com)
6   Russel Means — See (http://www.russellmeansfreedom.com) and Wikipedia
    (http://en.wikipedia.org/wiki/Russell_Means)

and Grandfather Martin,[7] speaking for the Hopi tribe. I was able to speak with both of them privately, among others. Who hosted this gathering? Dr. Chet Snow.

At the conclusion of the conference, a handful of attendees were invited to dinner at Dr. Snow's home, not far from the location of the gathering. At one point I was able to speak privately with Chet about his prior work. I told him that I enjoyed his book very much, but an obvious question remained. Without meaning to offend, I asked him, "How do you account for the fact that you were so far off the mark? None of the amazingly similar events that your subjects foresaw ever came to pass."

Dr. Snow must have been asked this question before, because he responded without giving the query a second thought. "I have come to believe in 'divine dispensation,'" he replied.

Or perhaps, to borrow from a well–worn colloquialism, "when you see into the future, it changes."

Or perhaps, we humans can use free will to alter future events.

Or perhaps . . . God can change his mind.

Or perhaps, a combination of the above.

With this prior discursion it may appear to the reader that I am discrediting my own work before I even present it; though I make clear that I am not the true presenter and in my role as a transcriber, I cringe at the suggestion that it is "my work."

In actuality, I share with you (my dear readers) my nagging doubts so that you might understand why I went to the trouble of searching for the supportive synchronicities that take up the latter part of this book, "In Search of the Nexus Points."

Instinctively I sensed that if the astonishing events that were being foretold in my journeys had validity, there would have to be other recipients of the same knowledge. Sure enough, not only did credible "nexus points" surface, but this additional source information helped in providing a certain conceptual "glue" that helped in piecing together the entire puzzle together into a cohesive whole.

Finally, at some turning point in April, 2012, not only was I able

---

7   Grandfather Martin Gashweseoma — See (http://www.thedreammasters.org/hopi/ martingashweseoma.php)

to find what had been transmitted through me as highly credible, but I became (though it took months to get there) a *believer*. I cannot say with absolute certainty that everything you are about to read will occur exactly as it has been related, but I have come to believe that the major points are a *fait accompli*. Moreover, I have come to believe that there are futuristic events which the free will of mankind may alter or even nullify. Then there are events over which we appear to have little or no control. Most of what you are about to read (I believe) falls into the latter.

Not that I expect you to accept anything you read in the chapters that follow with blind faith; in fact, I have been told that you should perform your own inner explorations so validation may come from within, a subject that is expanded upon later. One of the things that was emphasized to me repeatedly during my ayahuasca journeys was the importance of 'direct cognition.' In fact, we are about to enter an age of human consciousness where knowledge is obtained through direct realization, and not psychopathic, self-interested middlemen who have spent thousands of years telling people what to believe, what to think, how to live, how to raise their children, etc.[8]

A FEW WORDS ABOUT PRESENTATION

Most of the spiritual journeys taken in creating this book involve transcription, and a much smaller percentage involves memory. Originally, Cathryn transcribed the early work, writing down whatever I said to her during the session. Later, we used a voice recorder, after which a written transcription was prepared. All paragraphs which follow are in **"quotes and bold type"** and are direct extractions taken from the original transcripts. Additional text that is added to provide clarity is inserted *parenthetically*, but it is still in *bold*. Comments and questions by me and others present during one or more sessions can be found imbedded in the paragraphs, bracketed in *[italicized type]*.

You may also find that it takes time to adjust to the dialogue, which contains frequent shifts between first, second, and third persons, often within the same sentence. This resulted from my floating between my own position as subject and transcriber, the input of higher intelligences and even Source (wherein I surrendered to the point where subject and object are the same), and comments to those around me, not to mention instructions to Humanity. However, once you make the adjustment,

---

8   Thomas Sheridan – My revelations concerning this topic closely parallel the work of David Icke, who – quite interestingly – began his journey as a author/speaker on spiritual subjects after a profound ayahuasca journey in South America more than 20 years ago. Separately, one gets a better picture as to why our world leaders appear to act with such psychopathic abandon when reading Thomas Sheridan's *Puzzling People: The Labyrinth of the Psychopath*.

you'll find that rather than confusing the communication, it is somehow strengthened.

Along the same lines, readers should be aware that in virtually none of my ayahuasca sessions was I alone. As you go through the channeled quotations within each chapter, you will note that my wife, Cathryn Caton, acted not only as a recorder of each session, but a frequent questioner. The same goes for my editor, Jack Bracewell, who sat in my sessions from April 1 onward.

Another area of potential adjustment concerns gender. My experience of the ayahuasca plant spirit, which, as I recount in the book, has become quite deep and intimate (some might say it borders on the romantic), resides on one level where I experience "her" as feminine. And on a deeper, more power level of manifestation, the ayahuasca plant spirit is clearly beyond gender. Nonetheless, I chose to refer to "her" in the feminine throughout the text. Similarly, my experience of God or Source is (choose whatever word you feel most comfortable with to describe the boundless, absolute field that is the foundation of all relative Creation) one that is completely genderless. However, perhaps in keeping with tradition, I usually refer to the Creator as God or He. I offer many apologies in advance for any sensibilities this may offend.

Some will question the source of this material. The title of the book suggests that the information itself came directly from the ayahuasca plant spirit, whereas the plant spirit acted as a conduit to the introduction of other higher intelligences, and eventually "Source" Itself. In fact, my present experience of ayahuasca is that she has been the guardian of an important spiritual portal connecting human consciousness with the Divine for many millions of years. That this does not comport with modern anthropology is of no concern to me. Similarly, I am not persuaded to alter how I relate my experiences based on the current preoccupation of entheogenic research with the companion plants that supply the DMT (di–methyl–tryptamine)[9] or the DMT itself, a critical component of every ayahuasca preparation. DMT may provide the light and the visuals, but it is ayahuasca vine that provides the sound and the power. Without both, the spiritual experience — however euphoric — is incomplete.

I apologize if it sounds as if I've been evasive in identifying sources or have failed somehow to be more precise. As you go through the text, you'll find that Source doesn't want you to take my word for anything.

---

9   DMT See Wikipedia. (http://en.wikipedia.org/wiki/Dimethyltryptamine)

Your own heart[10] will tell you where these messages come from, and if you fail to connect with Source (pun intended), you have probably failed to connect with the Message. All true knowledge comes from within, not without. This book is of no value to you if it doesn't *ping a knowingness* that is already dormant inside you. However, the good news is that your decision to read this book is a good indicator that within your heart there is already a bell that has just been waiting to be rung. By the time you finish this book you should already have a good idea how long that bell has been there.

Another issue that arises whenever the topic of source comes up is the potential for meddling by the mediator, or the filtering of the message through the native bias of the receiver. The historical record of those who purport to have had Divine encounters clearly shows this. How else can one account for the fact that Christian mystics always see Jesus, or some other icon of their tradition; Muslims hear Allah; Hindus encounter Lord Krishna, etc.? One example of cultural bias is an ayahuasca journey I took outside of Tena, Ecuador in the Amazon jungle, where a shaman told me that I was very beloved by the Queen of the Forest. How could he possibly know this? Because she told him, of course! Embarrassed and feeling quite sheepish, I had to ask after the session who this was. Only by way of description was I able to gather that the closest archetype[11] to this indigenous, Amazonian divinity that I could compare in my own cultural tradition was the Virgin Mary, with protector/warrior overtones reminiscent of the Greek Virgin Goddess, Artemis.

So there is no time when I am "vision questing"with ayahuasca where I am not acutely aware of both my responsibility to faithfully communicate the "message" on the one hand, and my potential to culturalize, if not pervert, the message, on the other. Despite my best efforts at neutrality to present the messages as unfiltered as possible, I have no doubt that there are vestiges of the personality of Greg Caton that come through now and again. Perhaps this is unavoidable, even for the best "spiritual translator"; and for all I know this could be the seed of thought behind the Portuguese proverb; "God makes straight with crooked lines." Nonetheless, I have tried my best to stay out of the picture and let Source do the talking. Where I have felt the need to inject parenthetical comments, I have tried to make these obvious.

Along these same lines, it is important to note that while many excerpts in the book are "word–for–word" telepathic communications,

---

10   Heart as in *spiritual heart* defined by Irmansyah Effendi's — *Smile To Your Heart Meditations: Simple Practices for Peace, Health, and Spiritual Growth* (http://www. smiletoyourheart.org/)
11   See glossary.

there are many others that are attempts to put communicated "thought forms" into language. Examples arise to clarify points that are pulled from my own memory; while others, such as the use of the "Christmas metaphor" have been channeled directly from Source. Not everyone who reads the manuscript prior to publishing was comfortable with my "translations." In one instance, a close friend took issue with the use of the word "stupidity" in a description of humanity's current state of spiritual ignorance. "Would a higher power really use that word?" He asked. And I had to tell him that I understood his sentiment, and to a degree I sympathized with it, but I had only spoken what was communicated and chosen words to describe the thought–form communication.

In a minority of instances, there have been communications with angelic entities other than Source, and I clearly identify this in the book. Occasionally, this has led to the problem of objective identity.

For example, I had one session with a group of twelve angelic intelligences that spoke with one voice — not unlike the way that author Esther Hicks[12] describes her encounters with a collective entity she calls "Abraham." When I asked this group their name, I was told flatly that they had no name.

"Why is that?" I asked telepathically.

"Because we reside in a domain that in your spiritual literature you would refer to as 'seventh heaven,' and there is no use of language here. All beings are known and addressed by their distinctive vibration and all communications are strictly by thought." Sensing my frustration, they added, **"Do not even dogs on your plane fail to use names? Do they not identify each other, their master, and all other creatures by their scent?"**

I couldn't think of a sensible response, so I let the issue go. This was not a difficult thing to do because the information they later provided struck me as brilliant.

In fact, when you finish this book, you may be struck, as I am, with the problem of contemplating *why* the events presented wouldn't happen. Then, again, perhaps the paradox itself is our realizing that there is a Creator who is encouraging us to co-create a magnificent ending to our dualistic folly. That He/She already knows we will use our free will to assist in the creation of astonishing events that only appear to us to be predetermined.

---

12   Visit (http://www.abraham-hicks.com)

"Lo, soul, seest thou not God's purpose from the
  first?
The earth to be spann'd, connected by network,
The oceans to be cross'd, the distant brought
  near,
The lands to be welded together.

A worship new I sing,
You captains, voyagers, explorers, yours,
You engineers, you architects, machinists, yours,
You, not for trade or transportation only,
But in God's name, and for thy sake O soul."

~ Walt Whitman — "Passage to India"

Chapter 1:

The Ultimate Black Swan Event

> "You will experience a momentous event at the end of 2012 — where the perceptual boundaries that now separate the 3rd, 4th, and 5th dimensions will dissolve. What seem like impenetrable walls now will change to what will seem like transparent curtains."

In mid-November, 2011, this was the first communication that I received concerning anything involving the year 2012. Not that I was unfamiliar with the territory. Many years earlier I had read about the Hopi prophesies.[1] I was quite familiar with the work of Terence McKenna and his own ayahuasca journeys in the early 1970's. I knew well the deep significance he attached to this year in light of his thesis on "Timewave Zero[2]." Over the years I must have read at least 25 books that dealt directly with the supposed Mayan prophesies[3] and the end of their long-count calendar in 2012.

By the time of my kidnapping[4] in late 2009, I had pretty much given up on ever really understanding its significance. There was so much conflicting information on the market in books, articles, websites, and in the blogosphere, that any attempt to make sense of it just seemed like a waste of time. "Whatever is or isn't going to happen, just let it go," I thought to myself. I redirected my time and attention to my herbal work, finishing my hacienda, and working in my gardens.

Up to this point not once did 2012 ever enter into my entheogenic visions, nor did I express any intention in my altered states to want to know more, and then the message above was received unexpectedly. It was a particularly grueling night, because I overdosed with a pretty

---

1   Hopi prophesy see (http://www.tribalmessenger.org/prophecies/hopi-hopi.htm)
2   "Timewave zero", discussed in *The Invisible Landscape*, Terence McKenna. (See http://en.wikipedia.org/wiki/Terence_McKenna)
3   Mayan Prophecies — 2012 Phenomenon (https://en.wikipedia.org/wiki/2012_phenomenon)
4   Greg Caton was kidnapped on December 2nd, 2009 — (See details at http://www.meditopia.org/chap3-3.htm)

strong brew and spent the better part of the night either vomiting in a pail or bent over in pain on the toilet. When I first polished off the glass, my Shuari Shaman[5] looked at me in astonishment. "Greg, I forgot to tell you; I brought you, 'ayahuasca negra.' It's *very* concentrated, so you should only have taken a couple 'cucharadas.'" [6]

During a good vision quest I will get anywhere from one hour to five hours of verbal communications from the higher intelligences with whom I choose to speak. Some are angelic; some are extra-terrestrial; some are humanoids existing in a parallel universe that is markedly advanced from our time line, and some are surprisingly behind us.

But this night was different.

I couldn't identify the source of the communication, and it was the simple message you read above. Nothing more. This had never happened before. The universe is full of inter-dimensional beings that can't wait to sit down and chit-chat with human "psychonauts"[7] who are able to consciously navigate through their territory. But this communication was brief, discussing a topic I had never broached in my psychic travels, and it left more questions than it answered. It was as if my intellect was being baited to ask more questions on subsequent journeys, and that's exactly what happened.

On my next voyage, for the hour between taking ayahuasca and the onset of communications, I held a strong intentionality in the mind to know what the real meaning behind 2012 was. Not ancient, indigenous or urban legends, not theories; not some New Age promoter's meanderings; I wanted to know what was going to happen, and I wanted details. I knew that the course that a vision quest takes is strongly influenced by the intentions behind one's focus before the journey begins. What issued forth the second time was much more revealing:

> **"At the end of 2012 the Earth will experience a complete rebirth as it is passes through the galactic plane. This is not a theory. It is a pre-destined astrophysical event whose place in the time-space continuum cannot be altered. The 'Elite' on your planet are well aware of this impending event and is not discussing it with the public. During this event, the Earth will be subjected to energetic pulling effects."**

---

5   Shuari Shaman — The Shuari are a prominent tribe in Ecuador and Northern Peru. Though factions are separated by distance, they are bound by a common culture and language.
6   Cucharadas (one 'cucharada' equals 15mL or ½ ounce); tablespoon. See Ayahuasca in glossary for more.
7   See glossary.

At this point, I am visually shown the effects of this passage on photons, as all light in our solar system is sucked in the direction of the galactic center. All photons are made to appear like tiny iron filings being sucked towards a powerful magnet, or bread crumbs being sucked up by a powerful vacuum cleaner.

"The net result of this energetic condition is a period of complete darkness. This shall last for three days. Men shall experience darkness as they have never known it before, as even within a deep cave there is at least some photons emanating from the decaying matter and contributing sub-particles from space — some of which your scientists are completely unaware of. The more profound effects will be those on human consciousness. Although these changes will be occurring on different dimensions and planes simultaneously, how it will manifest on the gross third dimensional level is that human physiology will be subjected to a variety of frequencies — to energetic conditions — that will greatly expand human consciousness."

[Here there is a pause and I interject questions. "Hence this merging of the 3rd, 4th, and 5th dimensions I was first told about?"] "Yes. But this is just a tiny glimmer of what the experience will bring. The dimensions themselves do not change. What changes is human perception."

["Will all humans have the same experience?"] "The grossest physical effects, such as the three days of darkness will be experienced by everyone. But the enhancements to human consciousness will be experienced most intensely by those who are prepared. There are many who will experience little or nothing and I will expand on this when you are ready."

["What do you mean 'prepared'? How could one possibly prepare for such a thing?"] "By opening the heart (and) by working on the opening of the heart chakra[8] — because at its core this event is all about spiritual awakening. In fact, no event has ever happened like this before, since the beginning of Creation."

---

8 Chakra — (in yoga) any of the seven major energy centers in the body. The Heart Chakra (4th chakra) is the center of feeling, and the location where the True Self resides.

["Wait. Doesn't this event occur every 26,000 years? What are you saying? That nothing like this has happened in the billions of years since our Universe came into being?"] **"That's what I'm telling you. Stated in a conceptual framework you would understand, this is the ultimate 'black swan'[9] event. Its impending reality, nature, and purpose can be understood on the level of the heart. It can be 'felt,' but it is beyond the grasp of your present intellect."**

At the beginning of a journey I took on March 1, 2012, I happened to be privately lamenting how much I hated being on the earth plane. This thought-stream ended with my saying out loud, "How could God let this become such an evil place?" In response, I received:

"You will know why things had to unfold the way they unfolded. There was no other way to do it . . . as it pertains to 2012, it is an astrophysical event. But behind it there is a huge spiritual impetus being set by the Creator. There is the physical event, yes, but behind it is this huge spiritual unfolding . . . the subtleties are more important than the galactic passage itself."

With subsequent journeys, it became apparent that this wasn't a random astrophysical event. There was enormous intentionality behind it. It also became apparent why Source was waiting until the *last minute* (well into 2012), to reveal this information, and why so few people had received significant details until April, 2012. In fact, even from November, 2011 to April, 2012, it was obvious that crumbs of knowledge were being dropped in sequential increments, as if Source didn't want the "big secret" to get out prematurely. In the same March 1st journey, at one point I commented:

"Oh, this is interesting: God can feel pain. Feel separation from His Creation. And so, enough is enough. This experiment is over. Only Love brought Creation into existence. God wanted His love to be manifest. His cup was overflowing. 'I want My creatures back. I want them to know My Love, and I want them to love Me back. I am tired of where this has gone.'"

And then later in the same reading when I was pondering what the Passage would feel like:

"We don't have (experiential) reference points . . . (it's) a glorious new beginning . . . they (higher angelic beings) can feel our heart breaking and not wanting to be here. They

9   See glossary.

can't blame us. But stay the course. It is hard to believe this is going to happen. (But) be of good faith, good cheer. The rescue troops are on the way. They understand how out of control things are. When the Creator let things go, He Himself had to have a certain detachment. Sympathizing with what you had to go through. But you should find solace in knowing that this is a complete game-changer, the end of 2012. *["Why do we have to wait?"]* Certain events have to coalesce, like making a soufflé."

Over several weeks, the relationship between the Creator and his Creation was a constant, unexpected theme:

"I can't believe what you guys have done. You are so far out of sync, that it pains Him. He's actually in pain to see how much we have done to screw things up. You have destroyed the meaning of Creation. You're cut off from why there is a Creation in the first place. You don't realize how far out of sync we are with the joy, love, and energy that caused Creation in the first place. The world will feel different after this. It is this great cleansing. The energies will be provided, guided by the hand of God."

"It's okay to cry. To experience/appreciate what we've lost. Let go. Our spiritual development will have to be letting go of all these constructs to make life semi-livable. We have to deconstruct. True joyful living is much simpler than we're living now. We have complicated the Divine order of things."

At one point I pondered the paradox of a God who would issue forth a magnificent creation out of Love and Joy and then allow it to diminish to a point where it felt He was completely absent from it — and *then* wait until the last minute to reveal Himself. It made no sense to me. Later in this same session, this is an excerpt of what I received:

"God aches to have us know why things had to develop as they did. He wants us to share in the big secret. Compare this to a child opening his Christmas present. It's a joy to watch the child run up to the Christmas tree, open the gift . . . It would have spoiled the fun if you had said to the child, 'Look, I'm going to go to the store; (I'm going to) buy your gift (and guess what?), I'm really Santa Claus, so go under the tree and open your gift on the 25th.' It wouldn't be the same thing. It wouldn't even be closely the same thing . . . It's like the woman who loves a man and goes to all the trouble of making his favorite dish, lights the candles, wears something special . . . and she's not going to call him on the phone and tell him, 'I'm making your favorite dish, I'm lighting candles now,' and so forth. It wouldn't be the same thing. He had to keep it a secret and at the last minute go: 'Now do you see it all?' Not only that, you would not have cooperated through all these lifetimes, if you had known the big secret. You would have been useless. It's like, what is the use of reincarnating? You had to go through what you've been through to return to Godhead" or as stated in other sessions: 'You couldn't appreciate My Wholeness, My Light, unless you had (first) seen the dark.'"

The "Christmas metaphor" appears in several places throughout the vision quests. This one from the April 5th session:

"Still, honor Me in this. Everything unfolds in due time. Don't be so anxious that you have to open up your Christmas gift before Christmas. Just respect the unfoldment, because it's all part of the Plan."

This sense of finality is communicated throughout the sessions, this one from the April 5th quest:

"This is the end of time as we know it and experience it. What happens at the end of this year is the end of time. And He tells me if you ask yourselves in your Hearts, 'Is this the end of time?' you will get a resounding affirmation. Could this be the end of time as we know it? Ask yourself. Source says, 'Start getting into the habit of getting your news (i.e. information) straight from Me.' Ask yourself; 'Is this the new beginning that my heart has been aching for, for countless incarnations.' Ask yourself. And what God is saying is, 'I will give you the affirmation, so that you may know unto yourself, so that you may cognize that this is about the Return. You, aching for answers, over untold incarnations — and Me waiting billions of years to get you back.' He wants each person to know that and acknowledge it without anyone coming in between Source and His Creation. He's tired of the game. And because He is the Creator, as unlikely as it seems to us, He has the power to wave his hand, as it were . . . He is the ultimate referee of this game. He can determine when enough is enough. And it would appear that He has determined that 'enough is enough, let's go Home.'"

And later . . .

"THE MOST IMPORTANT THING I HAVE EVER TOLD YOU: What

happens at the end of this year is a lifting of the veil. Every person on this planet is enlightened (even if they don't know it). It's the most natural state of being. There is nothing more central to our nature than being enlightened. Only through this whole folly did God allow us to have a veil over our eyes. At the end of this year, we'll have this sense . . . 'it's so simple'. Enlightenment is the state of greatest simplicity. There is nothing more basic to our nature. What happens is that God is going to allow us to have it. Enough. It has reached (the end) point. People who (have a) complete absence of God. That's what this world feels like, complete absence of God. Every one of us is a manifestation of Source. But, despite that, those who do not accept are not going. You can accept or not. You must choose the Light; It will not force Itself upon you."

After the event itself, this became the second most dominant theme of the readings: the issue of choice. Preparedness determines outcome. To borrow from a famous Aesop fable, the experience of winter is different for the grasshopper than it is for the ant. Rather than being strictly a passive event, our internal preparations will apparently end up determining what we gain from the Passage, which is the subject of our next chapter.

"Stop this day and night with me
And you shall possess the origin of all poems,
You shall possess the good of the earth and
sun . . . . There are millions of suns left,
You shall no longer take things at second or
third hand,
Nor look through the eyes of the dead,
Nor feed on the spectres in books,
You shall not look through my eyes either,
Nor take things from me,
You shall listen to all sides and filter them from
yourself."

~ Walt Whitman — "Song of Myself"

Chapter 2:

The Role of Divine Responsibility

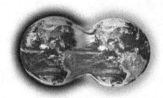

"It's about preparing internally . . . Preparation is mostly internal. Hold the experience. Normally we just go through life and what we remember, we remember . . . we get impressions from family and friends and circumstances, and so it's a very passive thing. Have remembrance. There is an effort in terms of willfulness. This is not just a passive thing where we go, 'Oh my God, certain things happened.' We should have it in our heart . . . this will not happen again. Remember this. Hold it special in your heart. It's a special event. Hold it. Remember it. And somehow in the remembrance of it, there is a certain facet of our relationship with God that is actually strengthened. I don't even know what that means, but that's what they're telling me. Hold it in your heart. Say to yourself, 'I want to remember everything.' There will be people who go through this and don't remember much. . . and don't appreciate it, and that's very sad, because this is a very big deal. They're saying to me; look at it from God's point of view, He let Creation go and it got so screwed up that when He provides this enormous gift, His own creatures can't even appreciate it, because they've been so dumbed down."

At several points during my ayahuasca sessions, Cathryn asked about preparations. When something this dramatic happens, what comes to mind when people mention "preparations" are things like extra water, storable food, medical supplies . . . physical provisions. But repeatedly whenever the subject of "preparations" came up, the guidance was invariably directed towards psychological, emotional, and spiritual preparations . . . which in the Mind of God all appear to be one and the same. This was a recurring theme, communicated from several different perspectives.

"You are going to have to take the various parts of what you regard as self . . . your five senses, your ego, the various parts of yourself . . . this is why some people will go insane . . . you have to take the reins of the horse . . . it's going to get crazy. So you must take the reins of the horse and let the horse know that you are the master. You have to hold it together . . . at the same time you have the desire to experience all of this. Things are going to be fragmented for a while; things are going to get very chaotic as this happens."

Whatever energetics humans are subjected to, this must be an important point, because it came up in several readings:

"(You) already have supplies. The rest is mental. Discipline, we must have going through this. We won't understand what it means until it happens. Remember their advice, so that when things happen, you will recall it. We are going to have to have a willfulness to hold it together. Like riding a horse. The horse has been trotting along for 6,000 years. And you're lazy. You haven't developed any of your mental skills. Now the horse is speeding up. 'Now you better run as fast as Secretariat.' Unless you're trained to be a good horse rider, you're gonna lose it. You're going to go insane. Like most of the people are going to go insane. You have to actually put energy into holding the reins as you go through this; the qualities of fragmentation as you pass through the galactic center. There is a willfulness that must be directed from within you — to keep and hold everything together."

Cathryn reports that as I passed this message along from the Divine, my entire upper body tensed up and I had my arms extended, while my hands held tight to imaginary reins. This Passage, along with others, appears to point to certain characteristics of the Passage that do not favor a lazy or unprepared mind or heart. In another passage, it was advised that it would be best to stay inside for the duration of the three days . . . and I got the distinct sense that it would be best to remain, as much as possible, in a meditative or prayerful, but still very attentive, state, not a passive one.

Moreover, other communications indicate that there are other opportunities that accompany the Passage:

"As we pass through the Center: just as we see our 'past life review' after death, there will be opportunity to experience not only own past LIVES review, but the past of humanity coming

UP to that (time). The memory of what we have collectively been through. Without that experience we would not be able to understand the totality of why God would have allowed this to happen in the first place. It is as if God wants us to understand why he would allow us to have such complete absence of Him. So instead of being just an individual past life review, we have to pass through this with a collective review. *[I'm getting all these amazing images from history.]* To understand the totality of where we've been and why we had to go there. It's like, the veil has to be lifted, and to do that, there has to be not only the review of what we've been as individuals, but what we've been collectively." And then later in this session: "It's about understanding this life. It's about understanding all your previous lives, going back to your separation from the Creator, when you were created."

In another session, the subject of a collective "life review" comes up again:

"The past of every man is filled with darkness. We all have dirt on our hands. Forget the past and looking into the darkness. You don't focus on the dirt when you clean your clothes . . . We will see all our past lives. But for those who are open to it, we have the opportunity to see where we've been, and where we have come as a species, and why it had to be."

And yet it would appear that this experience is by no means automatic:

"It's like that scene in *Private Ryan* (the movie), earn this. I will remember everything. I will keep drinking it until , I'm full. Appreciate this unique gift, this salvation from the hell to which we have descended. And earn this. You can earn this by sharpening the mind and saying, "I'm full. This involves a certain (discipline) of the will that is not (exercised) in day-to-day life, because people consider memory to be a very passive thing. We're lazy, and they're telling me that. We're lazy. Had we not let our psychic muscles go and become undeveloped, they just atrophied . . . It's shameful what you people sacrificed. The Creator, I wanted to see where this would go. So it's not like He blames us or anybody in it, because He had to see for Himself where his own Creation would go."

In the March 1st reading, the concept of "earning this" is further extended:

> "Prior to the Passage happening we should be cultivating a certain celebratory mood. You'll facilitate the birthing of it. It's like; your expectation of it (affects the outcome). God is actually asking us to be co-creators. Realize that this is the awakening. This is your time. He's not wanting it to be . . . like we just (insouciantly) put cat food in the (cat) dish. Have some respect for it. Cultivate this kind of celebratory mood, in the sense that we co-creators will help create a world that is renewed. It needs to be renewed."

Helping to "birth" in a new age on the New World is repeated in the April 3rd reading:

> "We are the parents of this Sat Yuga[1]. We are the ones who are birthing it in. Our job is to co-create with God to make it happen. [Jack: "How can we help?"] We can help by following our dharma, following our mission, what we agreed to. Feel your way into your place. Every single lifetime you had prior to this moment contributed to what you are now and what you are doing to make this happen. Everything that came prior to this had a purpose, even though we don't understand it. Remember, about the collective remembering. A life begins with the agreement to enter; it ends with the life review."

The April 3rd reading contains another passage that expands upon this theme:

> "We will be encouraging others to participate and be midwives, helping birth into existence a full consciousness of Wholeness. Whatever inconvenience we have, it is insignificant to the goal itself. People will ask if they should take ayahuasca. Soon enough things will reach a point where it won't be necessary for *anyone* to take an entheogen." [Jack: 'Would I benefit from taking ayahuasca?'] "Yes, it would help certain things perceptually, but only in the short term. The passage through the Center, whatever frequencies humans are subjected to, it's bonus time. This is going to bring about . . . the windows of perception just explode open. Whereas I am like a person with the door open 'two inches versus one inch' — I can see more than you can, what is that compared

---

1 Satya Yuga — See Wikipedia (http://en.wikipedia.org/wiki/Sat_Yuga)

to God opening the door completely? Then everyone gets to see. We're parsing smallness (here), compared to something so big we can't even imagine it."

The Divine acknowledges that this is made particularly difficult by our current circumstances. The following came out on April 3rd after I asked to experience the Passage as a "feeling," since I wasn't able to understand it intellectually:

"(There is this) enormous feeling of completion. (It) feels very round. And then it's done. We're on the precipice of it now. We cannot even appreciate what it means to be this close. It is like being on roller coaster ride at Disneyland; (but) we're blind-folded so we can't enjoy the journey. We're not able to appreciate what came before us, or why it's taken this shape, or this form, or this path. We're not able to appreciate it. We're just going through the roller coaster ride blind-folded."

At times I would be graced with mere glimmers of what the "post transition" state felt like. At one point I was frustrated because I had to work harder to speed up my vibration to stay in communication and I lamented after I reconnected:

"We are so far living in the muck, we don't know how far down we've gone. When this thing ends, I can tell you that we will look back on this now as an ugly, ugly (past). We're going to reach a point where we're going to have a sensation where — even on a soul level — we won't understand how we were ever able to tolerate it. It's the only way I can describe the feeling. How in the hell did we ever . . . on a soul level we're going to ask ourselves this . . . how did we ever tolerate this? That we so distanced ourselves from Source. How could we live in incarnated bodies living in an environment that was so removed from Source?"

At another point, Source emphasizes that despite the effort from the Divine, there are souls that are not going to "make it." So my associate, Jack Bracewell, who was with me on the session of April 3rd asked how we could help "other souls" prepare:

"There are souls who are not coming with us. *[Jack: "How can we help the souls to prepare; the ones that can come with us?"]* They are answering the question, but not the way you want it answered. You have to learn to feel the *flow*, as even a blind man in a river can *feel* where the center of the river is, where the current is the fastest — you have to 'feel' where the Divine wants to take this. Instead of thinking your way through it, you have to feel your way through it. By following the current, the Divine will take care of what it can, but know that there must be willfulness on the part of the soul. God will never say, 'You're coming with Me whether you like it or not.' He will never do that. So those souls who know what's going on have a will . . . they must invest of themselves. 'I am open to this. I understand this. It is time to go Home.' After eons and eons of screwing around, it's time to go home now. And, yes, thank you God, for showing us the contrast, but now it's over. It's done. It's so done . . . And God knows it."

In this same session, Jack, sensing the degree of Divine Authority, asked if it was "the Creator" who was speaking, and even in this answer, further comment is made about the "post transition":

"Not only is it the Creator (speaking), but all the other intermediaries were Me all along (i.e. the angels and other higher intelligences themselves were only acting on behalf of the Creator.) There is no existence without Me. If you take Me out of the picture, there is no existence. Ultimately 2012 is about the experience that it was the ONE all along . . . that all the different fragments were an illusion. It's a profound experience. The feeling is of profound interconnectedness."

Over time the ayahuasca sessions (vision quests) appeared to take on a progressive character, with each lesson building on principles established in earlier ones. An additional feature of the sessions, as you will see throughout the book, is that they became sharper as 2012 progressed. It was repeatedly made clear that this was deliberate. Certain things weren't meant to be disclosed, to anybody, until we got closer to the end of 2012. As it pertains to the subject of "divine responsibility," it was made clear that a certain state of mind would have to be held while experiencing "the Passage." The next lesson in responsibility graduated to "cultivation of the heart" throughout 2012 and up to the time of the Passage.

"This coming event is a harmonic of the act of Creation itself. In time and space, we hit this harmonic (that) has never happened before. It is a special thing to reenact the conditions of the original Creation. Those whose hearts are open will be given the opportunity to feel the same feelings that God had when he made the decision to usher in Creation. We can share this with Him. It is the meaning of (one of) Christ's parables. God wants to have a party, and He's invited us. And He'd like us to accept, because He'd be lonely without us. It's as if God doesn't want to be alone. He's lonely because we left Him. You have to know what Love and Joy it took for God to unfold Creation. Not out of a sense of lack. He did it out of fullness. He had such fullness; He couldn't hold Himself back from wanting to share it. We can experience that fullness (such) that God will say, 'Let me finally share with you why I did what I did. You'll understand in the end why I had to keep it a secret. It is time for Me to finally share it with you. And I've gone through such painstaking preparation; it would be such a sad thing for you to miss the party.' AND THAT'S THE MESSAGE. That is the Gospel of 2012 . . . It's the biggest Party Invitation in the history of the Universe."

As we first saw in Chapter 1, this "waiting until the last minute" to share the "big secret" is a constant theme in the readings:

"Evil has no chance in this because evil doesn't understand that it has no existence without Source. They (the Elite) only had power for a little while because God chose that they should have it for His purposes. It's over and they can't understand that . . . Everything will be made clear. But keep fostering love from the heart. Try to feel the love for your children; try to feel every sense of what you've known love to feel like. From the standpoint of human love, multiply that a couple million times, and that is God's Love. It pains Him that we are oblivious to His Love or its potency. He couldn't have done what He did without keeping it a secret. Your little girl may beg you to know what's under the tree, but it wouldn't be the same unless you wait for Christmas. It wouldn't be the same thing."

From the April 5th session onward, the theme of cultivating Love from the heart as it relates to one's divine responsibility only intensified. When asked what is the key to unlocking one's heart? This was the response:

"That I want you to have a full understanding of what you are. That I have such an enormous Love and Bliss for you that I want to you share in that Love and that Bliss. The same Love and Bliss that guided Creation. The same Love and Bliss with which I watch everything you do in every moment. It is the longing of a lost lover that you never knew about. And it's your Creator, and He just wants you to have just even the smallest reflection of the enormous Love that He had when He created all of Creation, but most importantly, when He created you!"

"That is the lesson of the heart. The lesson of the heart is appreciating the enormity of the Love of the Creator. If one could truly grasp that, there is no other spiritual path needed. There is no other meditation needed. There is nothing else needed. If one could only grasp the enormity of the Love that the Creator has for His Creation. And to have that and to focus on that, the love, (just) the love. If you want to reduce it to something as profane as to 'how do I get my ticket.' That's it. That's it. (Know) the Love."

And later:

"So Source is saying — lovingly — this is a *game-changer*. We all have old modes of thinking that we'll have to replace. Focusing on the Love through the heart helps the process of nullifying these old thought forms that we're very comfortable with, that have been with us for a long time . . . But they now have to be replaced. Quite apart from the idea that this is your ticket, the act of receiving God's Love and realizing that we belong to Him, that our place is with Him, that we're going Home now . . . that's it."

A private, personal question that my wife asked me ended with the following, seemingly unrelated addendum:

"On a heart level, if you're able to do enough heart work, you will know the rightness of this. You're not having to rely on me telling you . . . God wants to get rid of middlemen and that includes me. God wants every person to know that they have a direct link to the top. They don't have to go to anybody. This is the end of middlemen. The end of intermediaries. This is about each person realizing that they have a direct relationship with God. And there need be nothing in the middle of that. And that's what's going to make life on this ignorance. And this (New) World is all about enlightenment. And there's just going to be no place for evil to get a toehold."

Source apparently understands that we have lost the psychic tools to be able to dig ourselves out of our current hell, which may explain why the coming "passage" feels like we're being thrown a "lifeline" from above. This understanding is reflected in the following passage:

> "(Feel the) flow of creation (and make a) habit of feeling your way upstream. We have to regenerate (the) subtlety of feeling. We've lost touch with our pristine origins. Like *Matrix* (the movie), where you have to be nurtured to regenerate the muscles (that have long been out of use). We are just like Neo. We've been sucked off for so long. Complete absence of God. What makes it worse, we've lost the tools to escape or modify it."

Still none of the messages from the April 5th reading gave anything more in terms of practicality. So Jack asked, "Is there a specific prayer that's simple . . ." and I telepathically picked up the rest, ". . . that will connect people to heart; I already get it . . ." A concrete answer followed:

> "We are entering into a time beyond words, because *words* are middlemen. Words have vibration. Words have their own spirits. It's all in the spirit realm. So what God wants is, forget the words. Love is beyond words. Focus on the feeling and stop thinking you have to use words for the prayer. Let the prayer be the Love. Let the Love be the prayer. *[Jack:"Prayer without words"]*. Prayer without words . . . (Jack), Source is feeling your yearning to have a more concrete answer. So here it is. Here's your answer: That God so Loved His Creation that He was willing to separate Himself from it and experience a pain that even unto God, you cannot begin to understand . . . solely so that we could know Him. That even the Creator was willing to experience a pain because His Love was so great for us. That He wanted us to know Him and love Him back. Like a lost lover. You can't know what I'm feeling right now. The yearning, the enormous yearning. I'm seeing this circular . . . you see a lot of shapes when you're on ayahuasca . . . this spiral with everything returning to Source . . . going back to center . . . going back to the Source. Maybe we could put THAT in prayer form and to focus on the heart. 'That God so loved me . . .' I'm being told that this is where Christianity

got its power from. It was a co-optation of that. 'That God so Loved the world that He gave his only Begotten Son.' Okay? That is a reverberation or a harmonic of what I'm telling you now . . . but unlike the Christian message, I'm giving you the original. *[Jack: "That we are all sons and daughters. It wasn't just the Christ."]* That God so loved each and every one of us that He would be willing to go through the agony of parting with us just to enhance our experience of Him. Where that experience of Him was what gave birth to Creation. This is about finishing something that started billions of years ago. As unlikely as it seems."

And then the intention from Source was returned to a "feeling prayer."

"'That God so Loved me and held me so precious that he would go through billions of years of pain to get me back.' And if that doesn't strike a cord with Source then there's no hope for them. That's kinda more my words than his. So I'm just giving you interpretation of feeling. If they can't see that, out of all His Creation that I was so precious that He would go through billions of years of painful yearning to get me back . . . Can you ever say that a human lover could love you that much? . . . So, that's it. So that's what we give to people. And that transcends all techniques, all forms of meditation, everything. That's it. *[Jack: "So when I feel this yearning in my heart for Source . . ."]*. That God Loves you — individually. That God so Loved you individually that He would go through billions of years of aching and yearning, to get you back. That's it. You want to know how to fulfill your (pre-incarnational) contract and get people onboard? That's it. And, again, you must be detached from the result. You must give your effort, act in the Loving Spirit of the Creator, but you must be detached from the fruits of action. You can influence your action all you want to . . . this is what it says in the Gita. You cannot predetermine the RESULTS of your actions. You can only influence action, not the fruits of action. So, we have to go through this with a certain detachment."

"This is going to be very important as we go through the . . . oh geez! . . . *[Cathryn: "What are you seeing?"]* . . . What I'm seeing is this . . . it's like the analogy of the horse. Everything is being sped up. The talking about it is entirely different from the experience of it. As you go through this, you're going to feel like you're on warp drive. It's why certain people are going to go nuts. And this is part of preparedness. You have to be . . . God's Love is the thing that insulates us. How do I say this? The danger of travelling that fast? To be invested in His Love is to be protected as we pass through this. Because if you're not in this cocoon of Love as we pass, it can psychically rip you up. It can do some pretty mean things . . . If you want to get through this in the way God intended it has to be with a fully embracing of God."

Later in this same session this thought-stream was expanded:

"To understand everything Humanity's gone through, to understand everything creation's gone through, there have been progressive stages; there is an importance to having this understanding before you go into it (i.e. the Passage). Having the knowledge of certain things before going into it, will make the experience entirely different than going into it and being (ignorant): *[Jack: "because then you can have certain realizations . . ."]* and understanding God's Love and the need for completion . . . In and of itself, God's Love brings about knowledge of all things. That Love is the actual precursor to everything else (i.e. knowledge of all other things). Understanding and focusing on His aching and wanting us to come back to Him — in the act of doing it — a by-product of that will be that we will see things through God's Mind and we will understand why He's been doing what He's been doing, rather than now, we've been having to take His Word for all this. He wants us to understand that if we were Source, we'd be doing the same thing. He wants us to fully be in His Mind. I don't know how else to say this. He wants us to be full participants in the whole thing. And we can't possibly be full participants if we don't appreciate what He's doing and why He's been doing it. "

"[Jack: "I've been having this feeling in my heart, this longing . . ."]" "For whatever reason, He's giving us a choice because it's not Love if He makes us do it. It's only the return of His Love, if from our free will we say, 'I understand how much You Love me. I'm so honored You would wait billions of years to get me back. And I love You with everything I am capable of. I love You.' It's like a long-lost lover — as in LONG as you don't

understand the word, long. *[Jack: "I understand because when you said it I experienced it."]* So apparently what this is all about is, it's about coming Home. . . and speaking from the heart, 'For God so Loved me, that I was so precious to Him, that He would go through billions of years of agonizing separation to get me back, that I mean that much to Him' . . . and the thought of that, the meditation of that, that is it in its totality. That's what I'm being told. So you (Jack) wanted a method, you wanted a technique, there's not much more to tell as far as THAT goes. That's the totality of it. Source is emphasizing, it's simple. Don't disrupt the purity of it by taking something that simple and making it into something more complex. Make it easy, make it simple, because at the point of Creation, Source is saying it was all effortless, it was just a flow, like milk coming out of an overfull milk pitcher. There was no place else for all this Love to go. There just wasn't. Creation had to happen because He was just so full and had no place else to put it."

The simple technique, described as being supported by God's grace, is such that it appears to present a line of demarcation for those who don't "get it."

"If people say that and they can't feel something, then they need to go through the experiences (of the Dark World described in Chapter 4) . . . if they are closed to it or they won't do it or they won't perform it or they don't want to participate or any of the above, you need to be detached. It's their journey now, not yours. They still have experiences to go through."

This same concept is repeated in the following passage:

[Jack: "We need more details (concerning Divine Responsibility) so we can BE more responsible between now and what's to happen."] "I'm being told... don't make the meditations so complicated. It's the focus on the Love. Make it simple. Here's your message: that God was so Full of a Love and a Joy that we cannot begin to fathom. Out of that Love and that Joy, He had to Create. He had to let it out. It is the only way I can express what I'm being told. Our Divine Responsibility is to attune ourselves to the Love which is at the very Fountainhead of Creation itself. It's at the very core of why He created humanity

in the first place. What we, 'homo sapiens,' are a designer species. We're occupying bodies in long lineages (of genetic manipulation). Forget the Annunaki. We've been genetically manipulated for (many more) hundreds of thousands of years. So when I refer to Humanity, I'm referring to what we are as souls. Our spiritual entity . . . so the goal of divine responsibility is returning that Love to Him. He created us so that we could share His utter and complete magnificence . . . from God's perspective, everything is on autopilot, but from our perspective we're still struggling. The New Earth is where the (new) Satya Yuga begins . . . it looks to me, as impossible and as improbable as it sounds, there are those of us who go to the New World and there are those of us who go to the Old, or whatever you want to call the other planet . . . we have to become more detached. I am being reminded of a line from the Gita: Chapter 2 Verse 12; 'wise men grieve neither for the living nor the dead.' Because everything is . . . you're going to get it all. I promise. You're going to get the whole thing. You're going to understand why everything happened as it did. *[Jack: "When we go to the New World, will we be Home with Source?"]* Yes, you will have an intimacy with Source and with His Creation you cannot imagine. You will understand the Whole. It's the only way I can say it. You'll understand the Whole. You'll understand everything. But from here until that time . . . the line, as it were, that tethers us to Source. Even Source is not comfortable with that way of putting it . . . is it so hard to focus on Love? Are you so far gone that you can't get this? The line that connects us to this Event, to Source, to this New World is to understand this primordial Love. One cannot make it simple enough. God is in Love with us, and He wants us to love Him back. And there's an element of the *wishful Lover*. The Lover that is yearning for you to come back to her."

Repeatedly the point is emphasized that the sharing of God's Love is intertwined with the sharing of Knowledge, which is the result of exercising one's Divine Responsibility:

"Know that each human who's open of heart has the ability to be in His Mind to see things through His eyes, to experience His Joy, His Bliss, His Love, to actually partake of this birth of Creation . . ."

And apparently this sharing is far-reaching. The following passage concerns "parallel universes," a subject we'll discuss further in Chapter 4:

> *"[Cathryn: "After we go through the rift, will there still be parallel universes?"]* **There is this coalescing. It appears that if these other parallel universes did exist (after the Passage), there wouldn't be the singularity. And according to God, there wouldn't be much to celebrate."**
>
> **"Your experience of yourself will change because you, Jack Bracewell, have to be merged with all the billions of other Jack Bracewell's that are out there, so that we are all brought together.** *[Cathryn: "and we'll be conscious of all those experiences."]* **And for this cycle to complete itself, not only must we have conscious awareness . . . oh, this is all about our movement from the small to the bigger, not only will we have knowledge of this life and all our previous incarnations, but of all the other fragmented parts of our soul that have resided on all the other parallel universes. This is the complete, total understanding that comes at the end of 2012. (It is) a complete, total defragmentation of the Universe. Everything went out and got fragmented, fragmented, fragmented, and all of a sudden, in one event God is taking all of this expansiveness and He's just going, 'I want it back. Enough, I've waited long enough.' This is beyond any concept of improbability. (But) this is what's in the deck."**

And later:

> **"I'm also getting the sense that in a very nice, clean, satisfactory way (this Event) puts evil in its place. If this had been known about for a long time, evil would have longer (to respond). But being this close to the end, the sense I get is that God wants a very satisfactory conclusion. In His Mind, this is such a slam dunk. This is so conclusive. He wants an ending to the story that is every bit as grand and magnificent as He is. There are no words you could use to describe how much of a big deal this is. And it seems so improbable, but only because we've been laboring so long in a state of hopelessness. Feeling that (things) didn't feel right. We were subjected to conditions (for so long) that were so contrary to our loving nature. A lot of people will read this book and think, 'This is too good to be true.'"**

Throughout the readings, Source is emphatic that people should learn to get their information directly from Him, including a way to confirm that the contents of this book itself are not fabricated:

"You may test the veracity of everything in this book if you will simply go into your heart and say in all sincerity, with a deep, earnest, child-like desire to know the truth, 'Please tell me if this is true?' And what Source is telling me is — to someone who comes before Him in a state of child-like innocence — He will confirm to each and every person, 'Yes, this is true.' And they will know it within their own heart."

"Getting confirmation" or "getting knowledge" directly from Source is a common theme throughout the vision quests, even on matters of practicality:

[Cathryn: "After three days of darkness and a New World will we have access to free energy, teleporting . . . ?"] **"The problem is with the way that you worded your question. That you will simply have the desire, and (then) you'll have the knowledge. You don't have to be beholden to anyone or pay for the knowledge or whatever. You'll appreciate (the) powers of mind that you have (long ago lost). Again, they're showing me this picture. They are saying, your psychic muscles are completely atrophied. And what's going to happen is that this is going to have to be re-cultivated. You'll have to get used to the experience that the issuance of a thought by you, 'I want to know this (free energy),' could be whatever . . . that things got so dense on the third dimension and so fouled up that we've lost touch with the power of thought, with what a thought can do, what a thought is. And so when you say you want access to this or that knowledge, you will simply have the desire that you want to know this, and that thought will go out and you'll be able to have the experience of a thought going out and gathering to itself the energy, the information, that was the basis for why you issued that thought in the first place."**

The importance of willful preparation and confirmation to obtain the full benefit of the Passage was made even more clear whenever the subject of our planet's "Ruling Elite" came up — which is the subject of Chapter 3.

"Of persons arrived at high positions,
  ceremonies, wealth, scholarships, and the like;
(To me all that those persons have arrived at
  sinks away from them, except as it results to
  their bodies and souls,
So that often to me they appear gaunt and
  naked,
And often to me each one mocks the others, and
  mocks himself or herself,
And of each one the core of life, namely
  happiness, is full of the rotten excrement of
  maggots,
And often to me those men and women pass
  unwittingly the true realities of life, and go
  toward false realities,
And often to me they are alive after what custom
  has served them, but nothing more,
And often to me they are sad, hasty, unwaked
  sonnambules walking the dusk.")

~ Walt Whitman — "Thought"

Chapter 3:

The Relationship of Evil to the Passage

"There are evil entities whose very existence is in jeopardy as a result of this change. They are fighting for their right to exist. As humans, we (our spirits) are immortal; these entities are not. When they die, it is the end of their existence. They do not incarnate. The act of people 'waking up' is harmful to them. There is HUGE energy being placed on keeping people stupid."

The vast realms of non-physical parasitic beings who sit at the feeding troughs of human thought are discussed at various junctures during the vision quests, and was mentioned in the readings before the subject of their human equivalents every came into view. As the communications progressed, the relevancy of evil entities, in this and other worlds, became more and more obvious in relation to the unfoldment of 2012.

[Jack: "What are these evil entities? Can they feed off of . . . ?"] "'I am the Creator of all that is. I have given you a piece of Myself . . . Spirit . . . I created you with a part of My Own Heart and your heart is a piece of the heart of creation.' The Heart of Source is bigger than the heart of Creation. Because of that every human is a miniature God. When you put thoughts out, you attract beings who would like to feed off of it. Every human being is a piece of the Creator — a manifestation of an unseen magnificence. When you put these thoughts out, it attracts on the spirit realm beings that want to feed off the thoughts. This is how habits get started. Every habit has beings that will feed off of it. Every habit you can think of. Like people who are smoking, or even people who fidget with their hair . . . There are beings who will feed off of your fidgeting. There are beings who will feed off of nearly every human preoccupation.

"So to get back to your original question: These elementals are a certain class of evil spirits. But we create them, really. We put them into existence. Some of them are in existence prior. A great many of them we create with our preoccupations. They're parasitic. They just feed off of us. There's a whole class of these beings . . . that without us they don't exist. There are so many different beings that don't want this to happen. They have very nice, luxurious dinner tables . . . and now, dinner time is over. These entities can pass from one parallel universe to the next. They're porous. These insidious little creatures are everywhere. They reside in an unbelievable number of parallel universes. They go where they want. They think they're important, because in a way, they are."

The role of evil as it relates to the Passage was initially broached not from the perspective of extremely powerful people who exert enormous control over earthly affairs, but on the various evil entities who are created by human thought forms over time and exist on the astral planes. They feed primarily on human fear, anger, greed, lust, and other emotions — the greater the intensity and participation, the greater the feast. In return they can provide favors to those who seek power on the physical plane — individuals who will, in return for help from entities in the unseen worlds, do whatever they can to enlarge their dinner table, figuratively speaking. Only those at the very pinnacle of power in the physical world know how this works. The vast majority of politicians, well-placed government bureaucrats, corporate chiefs, military elite, and other little minions of darkness are completely oblivious to it.

Referring back to the passage above, this isn't to say that certain people in power don't have an enormous investment in keeping their people dumb, docile, and dependent — for a range of reasons that seem perfectly legitimate to them. But there are entities in charge that play an even greater role in the unfolding drama. This is made clear in the passage below, one of the longest in any of the sessions for a single given issue.

"That's why 'they're' afraid. When this thing happens, it comes with this momentous sense of the arrival of the Divine. That the more that one has been working with dark forces . . . oh, this is hard to put into words . . . they are exposed in a way that makes them look *really bad*. I'm getting the sense they fear more the sheer embarrassment of it. 'Cause the whole world's gonna know. The whole curtain comes down. It's like, show's over . . . they lose control of all souls that graduate to the New Earth (forever)."

[I direct a question myself] "How many know what I know? (pause) They're saying there's a thin crust at the top that all know this. They are obsessed with it . . . that is why we see what we see in world affairs. They are like heroin addicts. They're lust for power is so great, it's controlling them. This is beyond their control. They're going to go down with the ship. They are accelerating all this evil and chaos and everything else. It's like, and I hate to use this expression, Satan's last hurrah. They know the party is over, but they're thinking, 'We're not going to let the party end without finishing off the punch bowl.'

[Cathryn: "What do 'they' know?" (Repeating the same question)] "They know that the game is over. They are still hoping they can find a way out. Like a growing infection, there is discord between them. I see a small number telling the others: 'Why can't you just accept it? This is not something we're going to be able to (control). What we should do is accept the change that's going to be made and do what we're good at. Make the best of it to our advantage.' They are so locked into their matrix, they can't even break out. They've been doing this so long. Even though they're super wealthy and they live with all this privilege. They are themselves imprisoned by this cage, this thought (construct), they've been developing over eons, hundreds of years, through bloodlines. When they know this is going to happen, they can't even contemplate how they can break free of it and just open up to the Light. Those at the top of this thing have their own internal struggle. On some level, every being of higher intelligence knows what this means. We just don't see this because our higher faculties have been suppressed . . . with (industrial) fluoride, (deliberately constructed) bad educational systems, pollution, EM stuff, all intended to keep us from knowing who we are.

"The jailer is as imprisoned as the person they imprison. They are living in their own prison. Rather than being open, 'We're ready to transcend this and experience the conclusion of a very bad cosmic nightmare,' (they relentlessly resist). You've heard the Indian expression: 'Your first 30 years, you make your habits; your last 30 years, your habits make you.' Well, forget about the life span of one man. Think about belonging to a bloodline that has been committed, its whole being, to serving the dark side. That is an enormous, enormous thing to try and throw off. With each generation, they were just putting on more chains. They are so far down the rabbit hole. They are so far thoroughly committed. There is this kind of thing about selling your soul to the devil. That's more than just a figurative metaphor. When you want something and you need the assistance of the dark to get it, you are married to the dark side. It is like a marriage. There is this bond. Then when you take that bond and you cultivate it over generations, over hundreds of years — I'm looking at these people, these souls; they are super rich. They are the most powerful beings on earth. (*pause*) Oh man . . . they have all kinds of ET help! There are all kinds of dark beings . . . they become magnets for all these parasitic, dark beings on the non-physical realms.

"Yes, they are using these dark forces. They, in their ego, think that they are using these dark forces to get what *they* want, but they have no idea to the degree to which the dark forces have been using them to get what *they* want. And in that equation, the dark forces always get more out of the deal than does the individual. These people are locked into this prison of their arrogance because of their power and their wealth. They have had to use computers and psychically gifted people to investigate into 2012, because they are so far removed from having the ability themselves. They are locked — LOCKED — into this dimension, this earth. Few (of the Elite) are going to break free and get out of it . . . not at that level. Yes, there will be a few who break out, who see it, who will turn to the Light. But I am here to tell you, not many."

In another passage, members of the Elite are compared to actors who cannot distinguish between who they are and the characters they play:

[*Cathryn: "What about the religious extremists? (Be they) Muslims? Catholics? Mormons? Baptists?"*] "Each and every one of them has this opportunity, but they must be open to what is happening. (The) Pope must be free of the illusion of what he is. In our reincarnations we have *all* been actors.

This year we are getting to a point where we have to have the sanity to say, 'It was just a role. I was just being an actor.' The story of Richard Gere, continuing to stay in character at the Beverly Hills Hotel after his role in *Pretty Woman* was over, (whether true or not), is an example. The Pope and all these other minions of darkness don't understand this. If you're a Rothschild or you're a Rockefeller, you've simply been playing a role. But now its purposefulness has ended. They're like Richard Gere, 'Hey, wait a minute. This role's too good to be true. It can't be the end of production. I gotta keep playing this role.' And what God is saying is, 'Wake up. You had a role, but the movie is over. Now let it go. The film is in the can. Now, as a pure soul, understand where you came from.' But that has to be a conscious choice."

At times the prevailing attitude of the Elite in accepting their temporary role in the grand scheme of Creation is treated with exasperation:

"The Illuminati just don't get it. They are such peons. 'I allowed this to happen.' They were on stage. They won't get off. (It's) time to bring in the guys with the hooks. They played their role and now it's over."

And in the same vein, this excerpt comes from the April 5th session:

"This is the ultimate Singularity. *[Jack: "It's as above, so below. The one single thing that is, is Love."]* And all these little minions of darkness, they are so, so, so tiny compared to Source. They just don't get it. The whole run of them (those at the very summit of the global power structure) are such a small tool. They were just a mere thought in God's mind. They were just a thought. God had this thought, and there they've been sitting for thousands of years . . . so obviously if they're just a thought in God's mind and He doesn't want them around anymore. Guess who's going to win this tug-of-war? *[Jack: "Kind of a stacked deck."]* Yes, slightly. What I'm being told is, don't give them any mind. They don't deserve it. Don't give them any attention. When you give them attention or you fear them, you're doing what *they* want (not what God wants)."

Despite the admonition to not give the dark forces any attention, their role in Creation is portrayed throughout the readings as a necessary component in producing the Singularity. In one vision I saw a huge sheet of "negative film" — a complete distortion of reality, yes, but as every photographer knows, a necessary tool in the process of creating a "positive print." In another vision, evil emerged as the sand thrown into the mouth of the oyster, without which one could never obtain the pearl.

However, these metaphors speak to the place of evil's role in Creation, not its manner of operation. In *vision after vision* dark forces are seen as a shadow that attempts to mimic the forces of goodness, but always for its own end. It occurred to me how ubiquitous this observation was, and yet few of us ever stop to fully grasp its significance. It is always the sick psychopath that preys upon the good-hearted. Never the reverse. You'll never see a good-hearted person attempting to prey on a psychopath. This became clear in the reading of April 23rd, which revealed the nature of the "Anti-Singularity."

"Evil has no power of its own. The Creator has allowed dark forces to operate as a necessary means to fulfill His Plan. Every grand act of goodness has its evil twin — the co-optation of the Light for selfish ends, for the dark possesses no Light of its own. You can clearly see this in the history of your world religions. How much is organized Christianity a perversion of the true teachings of Jesus Christ? . . . Modern Islam, (is) a perversion of the original messages from the Archangel Gabriel? How far have the various branches of Buddhism gone to distort the original teachings of Buddha Gautama? You can clearly see this in the affairs of state. How far have government policies in the country of your birth (U.S.) descended to pervert the intentions of its Constitutional framers?"

"Therefore, as it relates to the Singularity, you should expect to see an Anti-Singularity, a grand act of co-optation which mimics the great Return, but is an enormous perversion of it. Can you not see this now? How else would you characterize your One World Order — a vision of unity that binds all the nations of earth under one central authority with one global currency, all arising not out of love or compassion for Humanity, but an insatiable hunger to unite all Mankind under an irrepressible system of global slavery and exploitation."

When I attempted to peer into the nature of the One World Order, realizing that I might have a better insight into the Singularity if I understood its "evil twin" — that a study of the "negative" would reveal details of its "positive print" — I was aghast at the comparative vision that emerged. Where there was an acceleration of Divine Grace throughout 2012 to prepare souls for the Passage, I saw its co-optative "twin" in the acceleration of the dark into global economic chaos. The wave of growing consciousness was matched by the dark forces' efforts to impoverish world citizens to the point where attention would be diverted from spiritual growth to basic sustenance issues. The use of the internet as a tool for enlightened souls to communicate globally was matched by growing efforts to neutralize free speech.

In numerous flashes of historic imagery the unvarnished nature of the Orwellian was revealed to me; the ravages of war masquerading as efforts to bring world peace; the stupefying effects of modern, compulsory education dressed as the heroic effort to enlighten students; and in a subject that is dear to my heart, the debilitating result of an explosion in the use of pharmaceuticals mocking safe, inexpensive, highly effective, and increasingly, illegal — natural remedies.

Energetically I was able to "feel" the rising crescendo of Divine Intervention as we proceed through the rest of 2012 "matched" by its dark counterpart. As the dark forces become more "desperate," you can expect to see the Anti-Singularity augmented by efforts to initiate world war, a mock alien invasion, or some other global act of grand theater in the attempt to hold Humanity in fear and terror. This development is expanded upon in Chapter 6.

As Jack said so insouciantly at the conclusion of one session, "We shouldn't expect anything less from the dark forces. It's their job."

"Earth, my likeness,
 Though you look so impassive, ample and
  spheric there,
 I now suspect that is not all;
 I now suspect there is something fierce in you
  eligible to burst forth . . .
 I dare not tell it in words, not even in these
  songs."

   ~ Walt Whitman — "Earth My Likeness"

Chapter 4:

Mother Earth Divides Into Two

[Jack: "What is the importance of the 'heart' as it relates to this transition?"] **"The heart is the fulcrum between the chakras, the energy centers of the body. There are three above and three below. It is the soul's spiritual center of gravity. I am not referring to the physical heart, as your anatomy identifies it, but the infinitesimally small point beneath the sternum where the heart chakra resides. Similarly, the Earth has a similar function on a macroscopic level. Physically, so small as to be seemingly insignificant on the cosmic scale of things, yet still it is of immense importance in Creation's design . . . it is the 'heart chakra' of the Universe. Just as the ill-health of the 'heart chakra' affects the spiritual health of the individual, so has the ill-health of Mother Earth had far-reaching consequences throughout Creation . . . your universe and those that run parallel to it."**

Most of my ayahuasca journeys allow me to enter into an altered state where I become clairaudient. I don't see anything, but I'm able to communicate freely with higher intelligences. However, I do have very clear visions when the communications call for it. Such visions involve no volition on my part. Whereas my own mother was clairvoyant without the use of entheogens, I am clairvoyant with the use of ayahuasca. However, this occurs only occasionally and at specific moments and at specific moments when it would appear that Source wants to convey something to me visually.

One unforgettable vision came to me sometime in January, 2012, while I was questing. What I was shown was an image of Mother Earth from outer space. It was either during or shortly after the passage, I couldn't be sure. As I looked down at the Earth, I saw almost through her, as if the Earth were semi-transparent. I saw what appeared like chromosomal spindles lining up . . . and then the Earth *split* into two

Earth's of equal size. Our Mother Earth had gone through some kind of energetic mitosis and now there were two "daughter cells." After the Split, the Earth on the right began to get brighter and more full of life force . . . it's difficult to explain (*see cover image*). It developed the most incredible aura, in shades of green, blue, indigo, and purple. The Earth on the left, however, became lifeless and subdued, changing into various shades of gray.

I found the vision itself intriguing. I remember Sir James Lovelock, the Oxford climatologist, who coined our term "Gaia" having made the statement that our planet has 18 out of 19 systems that would qualify "her" to be called a living organism. The system she is missing is reproduction. After all, Mother Earth doesn't have a womb or other reproductive organ, so she doesn't have offspring.

What was shown to me is that even this is incorrect. She can reproduce herself, but not in the gross physical sense in which we think of reproduction. In fact, her offspring never reside with her on our universe. They exist in parallel universes or other realms.

The experience of parallel universes is not something with which I am unfamiliar. In December, 1978, I flew to North California for a spiritual retreat. During this period I spent all day, for about two weeks, meditating and practicing yoga, and this was after having spent eight weeks prior to that at a prolonged spiritual retreat near Malibu doing the same thing. Towards the end of the retreat, I had my first "Brahmic" experience while performing Patanjali's "pole star" sutra. My breathing stopped, as I began to feel myself free-falling — even though I was sitting there motionless, meditating on my bed for nearly an hour.

Suddenly my head filled with the most incredible white light and with my eyes closed, I was able to "see" 360 degrees around me simultaneously. Most noticeable of all was the most intense euphoria I have ever experienced, which seemed to penetrate every cell of my body. In such a state of extreme bliss, I honestly thought, in that moment, that I had attained "enlightenment," as my experience matched so closely the description of this awakening as recounted in Dr. Richard M. Bucke's seminar work, <u>Cosmic Consciousness</u>. But it was not to be; not yet. A minute later, I opened my eyes, if only to see for myself that I had "come back." It was a depressing moment.

When I returned to my home in Los Angeles, I found myself going in and out of another world that was remarkably similar to my own. I first became aware of it in my meditations, and then in my waking state. I spent weeks trying to dislodge my consciousness from this parallel universe in which resided another "Greg Caton." The experience, which was particularly unavoidable in the dream state, was very confusing because my alternate self (who was the same age as I was, twenty-two), had particulars in his past that were 90% the same as my own. We shared nearly the same memory, the same looks, the same talents, but the 10% of "his" memory, where facts were different, was interfering with my identity in *this* universe. It became such a huge problem for me that although I was attending Cal State University Northridge (CSUN) that winter/spring, I eventually had to drop out. I just couldn't concentrate.

Years later, I asked my mother if she had ever encountered such a thing. She told me that not only had she routinely encountered other parallel universes (though she didn't use that term), but she had met 135 other "Greg Caton's" in universes other than this one, some of whom had already "passed over."

"You know, Mother," I said with a serious demeanor, "scientists say there must be billions of parallel universes, so how could there only be another 135 'Greg Caton's?'" My mother, who had the most child-like innocence of any adult I've ever known, apparently didn't realize I was joking with her. She looked back at me with the most pitiful, painfully apologetic look I've ever seen and said, "Oh, I'm so sorry, dear! . . . *I got tired of counting!*"

I began Chapter 1 with the most localized phenomenon that will mark the cosmic events that come at the end of 2012, an astrophysical event. But as the readings proceeded from March, 2012 onward, it became apparent that "the phenomenon of 2012" resided in non-locality, as well, and that it would affect the entire "multiverse." Most shocking to me was how central the events on Earth were to the entire event.

As I viewed the Earth "splitting" into two separate bodies in a process not dissimilar from mitosis, I was telepathically told the significance of the two bodies. The one that appeared lifeless and moving to the left on its own trajectory was the place where souls would continue to go who had become enamored of a God-less society. In vision after vision, not unlike the levels of hell that Swedenborg was allowed to view, I saw the Earth's present Elite, and their future incarnations, obtaining the very world that they and their bloodlines had worked so assiduously for countless generations to create. **"It will be the ultimate manifestation** of the old Portuguese proverb: 'When God decides to punish men, He gives them what they pray for.'" I saw continuing wars, ending in a thermonuclear exchange, horrific Earth changes, and global pollution so bad that the skies appeared saturated with soot. And from outer space, I saw a planet that appeared all but dead. Except that it wasn't dead. It would be the new home for countless souls who had not prepared themselves energetically for the coming "Passage." And then I was told, **"If in their greed and selfishness 'they' so badly want a world that is bereft of the Divine, I shall grant them their wish."**

The planet whose trajectory took off to the right had an entirely different look and feel. It was absolutely radiant. Whereas the "dark planet" version of Earth appeared flat and lifeless, this one was bursting with life force, emanating a joyfulness that jolted the senses at the very sight of it. The entire experience was one of awe. Even in the vision state, I could scarcely gaze upon it. I wasn't sure whether this was because I wasn't yet ready to fully experience it, or perhaps because I wasn't yet worthy. I couldn't be sure. It was as if the Garden of Eden had reconstituted Herself, spread to every corner of this New Earth, and been allowed to regenerate the planet so that there was no place from her core to her outer atmosphere that did not radiate this irrepressible Bliss. So wondrous was the sight of this magnificent, celestial body that I could 'hear' myself talking through my own soul, visibly and silently weeping back in my physical body as I 'said' it: **"Oh my God! Let me be worthy of this! . . . Whatever I've done to offend you, I am so very sorry! . . . Do not forsake me! . . . Please don't leave me here. I wanna go home!"**

This experience occurred sometime in January, 2012, and what followed for the next several months were various revelations where the nature of this "Split" — as astonishingly improbable as it seems — was more fully explained. In the April 3rd reading, Cathryn asked me, "Is the Earth really going to 'Split'?" Out of the 'translation' of the thought-form, a response from the Divine came:

> **"Not only is it going to Split, but . . . the people who don't fully choose to embrace the Light, they are not even in our Universe. (It's) awful what they go through. People are about to make a series of decisions that (are lasting). There is great sadness on the other path. They have to go through the whole cycle all over again. '(Oh, so) you don't get it? Another 20,000 lifetimes for you!' They go off to a place where the cycle is repeated."**

Two days later, in the April 5th reading, she asks a closely related question:

> *[Cathryn: "Three days of darkness and the Earth splitting: so after the three days will we spontaneously have a direct link to Source?"]* **"Well, you should be cultivating that now, for even in this moment or in this room . . . I will keep asking you, 'Do you feel this?' Because what God is wanting you to do is (feel). He realizes that it's like you're a kid. You can't ride your bike yet; you still have your training wheels, and He allows for that. He understands that. But He wants you to make the effort. It's all about the discipline . . . this is the divine responsibility part. This is about 'I am making the effort. You loved me so much and now I want to feel that love. I want to feel what You have ached for billions of our earth-years to have back. You want to complete the circle. You Love us so much. And Your Love and Your Joy is beyond infinite and You want us to return it back to You, which is why You created us in the first place. So You want us to fulfill the real mission which is why we even exist.' And that needs to be the focus . . . the whole reason for existence is just to share in infinite Love. That's the whole reason we're in existence. 'Share in My Infinite Love . . . and complete the circle.' This is about completing something that has been not millions but billions of years in the making."** *[Jack: "Since before the beginning of time?"]* **"Hold on. What I'm being shown is, yes, because time is an artificial construct. This is the fulfillment of something that came from Source in the primordial thought that issued forth the Universe itself."**

Later in the same session, the full extent of the transformation described was put in even larger terms:

> **"This is happening not just in our universe. It's happening on all these parallel universes at the same time. Have we talked about this, Jack?** *[Jack: "No, but I know that it is."]* **(There are) vast, immeasurable realms . . . all these parallel universes. He created all of them, too."**

Apparently, these events do not happen all at once:

> **"Not everything is going to happen overnight. It's going to happen in stages. What I'm being told is that these three days of darkness are the trigger and many other things will follow from it that are corrective in nature. It's like Mother Earth herself needs a chiropractic adjustment after all this.**

She's been through hell. So I'm being told that you can think of many of the *earth changes* as Mother Earth's chiropractic adjustments. (Many strange) sounds (and frequencies) that people are hearing all over the world are (a prelude) of the adjustments."

And the effects on consciousness are not limited to humans.

In one session, Cathryn asked, "What happens to the animals?" Whereas there continues to be a degradation of biodiversity and an acceleration of species extinction on the "devolving earth," the New Earth experiences something entirely different:

"(This has) a profound effect in their own consciousness. Source is happy you asked the question. Our relationship with animals will change; more joyful. We will understand each other. There is this veil that is lifted. It feels like talking to animals (telepathically). They will understand us. We will understand them."

This led to a question about what plant and animal spirits "knew" about the coming Passage. The following is an excerpt of a very personal and uncharacteristically long response.

[Cathryn: "Do all plants and animals (i.e. their spirits) recognize what's about to happen?"] "All the animal and plant spirits know what 2012 is about. This doesn't mean the animals themselves are entirely conscious. But in the spirit realm, they know what this is about. In fact, she (ayahuasca) can read everything in my memory — you can't even begin to understand *her* power . . . there's a reason they call ayahuasca the mother of all plants, because you can't begin to imagine *her* power . . . so she knows everything in my mind. She can read right through me. And she's pulling out of my memory a poem and she's wanting me to recall it . . . 'Presentiment's that long shadow on the lawn / Indicative that suns go down / A notice to the startled grass / That something is about to pass.' (*Emily Dickinson*). What she's saying is that the spirit behind the poem that she pulled out of my memory sums up what's going on with the plant world. She is not comfortable talking about the animal spirits because that's a whole other realm. That's a whole other dominion . . . She'll cover anything you want to know when it comes to plants. She lords over the plant world."

[*Cathryn: 'So the plant spirits know what's going to happen?'*]
"Yeah . . . (it's) 'a notice to the startled grass that something is about to pass.' They know that the jig is up. That know that something is about to pass. So understand that plants have an unbelievable range of emotions. We belittle them, but you wouldn't believe how much plants know, even though they don't 'think' in the same manner that we do. But they have a range of feeling — again, it comes down to feeling — that is greater than the average person. Plants are amazing creatures. We've lost our ability to communicate with plants and animals. Ancients knew how to talk to their plants and animals. When they spoke to the plant, they knew they were communicating with the *spirit* of the plant. In an advanced culture that is not under the kind of Kali Yuga that we're under, the world around you is full of spirits. You're telepathically communicating with spirits *all the time* in an advanced culture. So, to answer your original question: yeah, they know. And in a way, they're happy about it because, and she (ayahuasca) is telling me this — modern man hasn't treated them too kindly.

"They are tired of being belittled and not being recognized for what *they* are. Plants feel, 'You may be the big cheese, but we're important, too. We give you food, oxygen, beauty, building materials, tools for spiritual development . . . we are your partners. What would your world be like without us? And yet look how miserably you've treated us . . . It would be nice if you respected us. It would be nice if you could somehow grasp how long we've been here and how much we know.' The Spirit of every plant on this planet has been around longer than us (Modern Man). (Even 'extinct plants' have spirits who mourn their lack of representation in the physical world.) It even frustrates the plants that Modern Man is so stupid. It's like 'everyone knows.' There is this hush over the plant world. 'Everybody' knows that something (big) is about to happen. (Yet) people are going merrily about their way . . . drinking Coke, watching baseball and 'Dancing with the Stars' and there is this huge, HUGE — you can't begin to imagine what I'm experiencing right now — this HUGE anticipation. You know, everyone is sitting in the audience. They're waiting for the curtains to open. They want to know what God's got planned because, in a way, God has even kept (this) secret from them . . . and so there's this huge anticipation for what's about to happen. And over here, you've got human beings who were supposed to have a special relationship with the Creator, and 99% of them are completely ignorant. Can you understand (from their perspective), how that feels? They're in amazement. They just can't believe we've fallen so far." And about twenty minutes later . . . "You can't understand the irony of the situation. (It's like a big wedding.) Everyone is there, but the groom hasn't shown up. Humanity is the missing groom. We're important to this party, and Humanity isn't there."

An unusual comment about the New Earth came when Cathryn asked a practical question: "During the three days of darkness, will candles still work?"

"(It is) possible to have (a) candle that works, but it won't work like you think it will. It will be dim, but this can be changed through thought. (The strength of) thoughtform will be increased. We have the impression in the 3ʳᵈ dimension that thoughts don't matter. We are in such density in our earth . . . (it) is so void of light, void of love, God, peace, harmony, joy. The most joyful people on the Earth right now cannot be compared to the least joyful people on the New Earth after this shift occurs. Because every single soul (incarnated on Earth) are living here in the muck. So it becomes a source of elevation. Whatever abilities we have now will be enhanced. Because, we're (now) living in such darkness."

Nonetheless, there is still individuality.

"There is still continuity. We will live in a place that combines the 3ʳᵈ, 4ᵗʰ, and 5ᵗʰ (dimensions). Our boundaries of perception will be greatly expanded. We will be able to use our mind . . . to travel psychically. (But) this event is not the great equalizer. This event will not make me an (avatar) . . . (but) the flow of evolution will be greatly sped up."

A question about reincarnation further elucidated the character of the New Earth, "Will this be the end of birth and death, or reincarnation, for all?"

"Your attitude towards reincarnation will totally change with this, because in the Creator's mind, in its pristine state, (Earth) was never intended as a place where you go to pay off karmic debt. None of that. What's going to happen in this New Earth . . . you can't believe the realm of spirits that are going to say, 'If you can't appreciate this, get out of the way, 'cause I want to go (reincarnate) in there!' Instead of being like right now, the angelic realms are full of (beings looking down on) . . . every child that's born, it's like, 'you poor soul, you're having to go down there (the current Earth)' . . . The answer to your question is this: we'll have to think of reincarnation in a brand new way. Birth will not be painful. Incarnating will be primarily about experiencing God's Love and Bliss (in a different way). *[Jack interjects the question: "Will there be a need for those who go to the New Earth to reincarnate again?"]* I'm being told that it will be primarily your choice. It won't be something you have to do. It will be a matter of choice."

At the beginning of one session, the following information concerning life in the New Earth came without any query, simultaneously referring back to social conditions in a Satya Yuga:

"Women are the foundation of society. They are the center of gravity of what makes a civilized society. They have lost their knowledge. Women have to be retrained to be women. (They) don't get proper training (as to how) to create a divine home. The rebuilding begins with the women, not the men . . . The Bible (story) is a complete co-optation of truth. It wasn't Eve that ate the apple to take us away from the knowledge of our pristine origin. It was men that mislead women, breaking long lineages of dharma. Birth was sacred . . . a child coming into the world! People are blind to this. Souls were welcomed onto the Earth. 'You are so special to us.' And there were always thoughts of love, thoughts of love, thoughts of love . . . so the child wouldn't be traumatized. 'You are so important to us.' In village life, this was an important thing. Every child that came into the world was a special event. There were no unwanted children."

Later, similar comments are made concerning conception as a harmonic of the larger act of Creation:

"Conception is sacred. A couple million sperm attempt, but just one is special enough to contribute to conception . . . Each incarnation of each soul is a miniaturization of the feeling God had when he created Creation. This is why God is upset with the misappropriation of the immense beauty of what sex and conception are. It is a diminishment of realizing how sacred it is. And it is something that is so powerful to experience . . . it is the specialness we do not appreciate, how important each and every creature is to God. Everything is a part of this immense physical whole. How blind we are to how perfect Creation was and what it meant to Him. How much His Love and Joy overflowed into the act of Creation."

Another practical question about the "New Earth" arose when Jack asked, "What about nuclear energy and other negative technologies? Will we still have to deal with that?" As you can read below, we will still have to clean up the mess inherited from our current conditions, but the clean-up will be done collectively and in a state of joy:

"(These are) transferred to the new planet. The question can be answered in two ways: this other (devolved) Earth . . . it goes off in horrific ways. It experiences all the things that Edgar Cayce talks about. The souls in the astral planes around that planet begin all over again. It's almost like go through way through high school. Imagine being 18 years old and flunking; and then you have to go back to kindergarten. You start over again. There is no place else to put you. (Currently) this is all beyond human understanding. (Returning our attention to the New Earth), we will still have the negative technologies in the New Earth. (But) if you have a dirty house, you just clean it up. Oil is part of Mother Earth's lymphatic system . . . Because of change of consciousness, we (will) do (the clean-up) all collectively."

After dealing with negative technologies came the following rendering, dealing with the remnant of human problems. As in so many of the responses to direct questions, the answers are unusually oblique:

[Jack: "Will we still have cancer?"] "There will still be the remnants of our existence, but with the change of consciousness, we will see it in a whole new light. Almost everyone will be a natural healer." [Jack: "I am feeling we won't need businesses."] "We will have an enhancement of our mental capabilities that is too difficult to describe." [Jack: "Give an example."] "Can you describe what a banana tastes like to someone who's never had one?"

But again, as we covered in Chapter 2, making the effort to be a part of the New Earth — one's divine responsibility, is never far away:

"(Going through) this Galactic Center is like getting on the big wave. (If you're surfing), you still have to paddle out, get on the board, and get inside the 'tube.' You still have to do something to get the benefit. The embrace with God must be mutual; the completion of a circle. At every point along a circle it returns to itself. We can only experience the fullness of what God is if we realize that we are the manifestation of how God returns to Himself. The circle is not complete unless we love Him back. All the joy and the benefits of life are about realizing that we are a manifestation of God, and whatever joy we can achieve in life is about realizing that God wants us, who are an expression of Him, to love Him back."

In another question, a few moments later, the subject of what would happen to serious drug users who didn't have the mental capacity to accept this challenge came up. The same answer was rendered:

"People who are on drugs and completely lost in it will probably be in the other universe. The embrace has to be mutual. You must be (able to) embrace Him back and say, 'Father, it's good to be Home.' You have to have the consciousness to say, 'I'm happy to be Home.'. . . (Drug addicts) are going to cycle all over again if they can't break free."

This principle was extended even over loved ones. At one point Jack asked what would happen to his son:

"You should attempt to influence your son. Even so, we can tell them *(i.e. our children)* what's happening, but, again, it's their choice. 'A prophet is never respected in his own home.'... As it relates towards your son, it mimics God's relationship with you. You can make the attempt, but you must be detached from the result."

The concept of remaining detached as it pertains to "loved ones" is expanded upon in this excerpt from the April 5th session:

"There are certain things that are just painful to know. That all of us have people we love that we won't be with (after the Passage). They have their own journey. So, in love, in love . . . allow the Creator to act through you. Allow yourself to fulfill the Divine Will. Make your desire, God's desire. And that's the flow. That's being in the groove, our desire and God's desire in the same way. You have surrendered your individuality to the Will of God. You are allowing God to just come through you. And there's your bliss. There's your destiny. And there's the fulfillment of the Divine script . . . when you have completely become a perfect instrument . . . when you see through God's Mind and you know that everything is the way it's supposed to be. And you won't have all these petty worries and concerns and doubts and fears and everything else, because those things don't exist in God's Mind. He doesn't have any worries or fears . . . He's just full. He's completely full."

The description of the "devolving earth" is every bit as intense, but is entirely different:

"They don't understand. This is spiritual suicide. God is going to allow them to experience what they want. This other earth will be transhumanistic .... a nightmare beyond George Orwell. It happens for millions of our earth years."

During the January readings, I was intensely interested to know how something so improbable could occur. My skepticism was never far away, to the point where I was having problems continuing with one particular session. Perhaps it was because the importance of the communication outweighed my inescapable skepticism that the Divine decided to throw me a bone:

"'Think of the flow of spiritual evolution as a river. Through the (flow of) rain, it receives its very essence from the sea, to which it returns. So does all of Creation flow through myriad twists and turns, only to return to Me, the Source. In contrary fashion, the activities of the dark forces act as a dam that has been erected for its own purposes. For a while the dam will prevent the flow of the water from proceeding . . . but only for a time. If the dam continues to prevent the flow of evolution from proceeding, the (ever-accumulating) water will find a way over or around the dam.'

"So have the dark forces on Earth acted to inhibit not only the spiritual evolution of Humanity, but because of this tender planet's central role in Creation, all other life forms, as well. Enough. In their ignorance, they themselves are initiating the 'Split' so the waters may return to Source. 'So that those who are ready for my Divine Love may return to Me . . . In my Infinite Mercy I could forgive the enormity of their transgressions, but

I will not force My Grace upon a single soul. However great the gift, the receiver must be willing to receive. And so . . . if it is hell that they wish, than it is hell I shall allow them to experience.'"

Quite apart from the literal communication of the reading, I was allowed to "feel" the effects of the contrary forces themselves. The force of evolution, involving the heartfelt desires of many millions of people who had had enough and wanted to return to Source, on the one hand, and the dark forces and those who were caught in its grip, on the other. It is a battle of Good versus Evil that is going on throughout the entire "multiverse," and it is this battle that ends in this enormous "Split" into the two earths. Or as I was told at another juncture in the April 5th session, **"You got all these beings that don't want this to happen, and you've got all these other beings that just can't wait to pop open the cork."**

The Divine understood that I would never be able to understand this phenomenon intellectually, as it seemed a complete impossibility. Instead, I had to experience its eventuality on the level of feeling, on a level of understanding that was deeper than mere intellectual constructs — in which all of mine were built upon a history of experiences that could never otherwise accept this "Ultimate Black Swan Event" as a possibility.

One of the most poignant aspects of this experience was my cognizing the sheer weight of the collective negative *karma* of so many members of humanity, having worked so assiduously to impede spiritual progress for their own personal gain. In its appearance and "feel" it reminded me of the water moccasins in Louisiana that attach themselves into these huge, round balls during mating season, a danger awaiting anyone who disturbs them as they bob beneath the warm bayou waters. Only this was many orders of magnitude larger and more malignant.

"Hast never come to thee an hour,
 A sudden gleam divine, precipitating, bursting
 all these bubbles, fashions, wealth?
 These eager business aims -- books, politics,
 art, amours,
 To utter nothingness?"

~ Walt Whitman — "Hast never come to thee an hour"

Chapter 5:

Awakening

By the session of April 5th, Cathryn and Jack became regular attendees to our subsequent journeys. Though I was the one taking ayahuasca, their roles became more participatory. The next scheduled journey was made for the 10th, so in keeping with our routine, I took about 60 ml. of my ayahuasca preparation at 6:52 p.m., knowing that communications would begin around 8 p.m.

Early in the session, I was greeted by a higher angelic being with an overwhelming, formidable presence. This entity wasn't Source, as there was a distinctive "personality," but it was powerful. Without even asking — something I simply knew by directing my attention — this was the Archangel, Raphael. The message that came forth was immediate and forceful:

> "Not many will come . . . our work is still extremely important, but the majority are not going. The importance of the exercises we've talked about is to help further inflame the desire to know God. There has to be this effort. This whole thing doesn't fall in your lap. There's this speeding up process. We're basically being given *the keys*. 'This is what's going to happen.' This is what you're going to have to do to get through it . . . with a sense of wholeness, not messed up. 'This is what's going to happen. This is what you're gonna do.' The vast majority are not going to listen, and many of those who listen are not going to follow the instructions, and many who follow the instruction are not going to do it with a certain rigor that's needed.

> "The reason he's telling me this is he's trying to impress upon me the importance of (this), and we're supposed to pass this on in some form or fashion to our readers or listeners that you must *stand up to this challenge*. Your challenge is make the effort of what's needed — to come home to God. It's time

to come home. But you must make an effort. Raphael felt it was important to make the (point) . . . that the effort must be made. It's not like 'voila' and it falls in your lap. Raphael is harkening back to something Biblical, 'Many are called, but few are chosen.' He also said that the Biblical story where the rich man comes to Christ and says 'Master, what good thing shall I do, that I may have eternal life?' And Christ says to him (and Christ already knew he was a wealthy merchant), '. . . go, sell your possessions and give to the poor, and you will have treasure in heaven. Then come, follow me.' And the merchant was stunned, and he ended up walking away depressed, and that's the background. That's when Christ turns to his disciples and says, '. . . it is easier for a camel to go through the eye of a needle, than for a rich man to enter the kingdom of God.'"

In a later reading, a similar Biblical passage is used as a reference:

"Enter by the narrow gate. For the gate is wide and the way is easy that leads to destruction, and those who enter by it are many.

"Now what Rafael told me is: 'There's a meme[1] there.' What Rafael was telling me was that there's a meme there between that story and what's happening here. Many are going to be called, and like the wealthy merchant, many are not going to make it or they're not going to listen or they can't give up their (earthly attachments) long enough to focus. This requires focus on preparing for the Return. There's going to be many who listen to our message and still aren't going to make it because they're not going to make the effort. I mean how many people buy books and they really don't read the whole thing cover-to-cover or read it in its entirety? Or don't get the message — the author's full message?

"(So) He says He's telling me this because it goes back to what Source told us the other day about attachment. We have to be detached from the fruits of whatever it is we're doing. It's a big thing. We're going to affect a lot of people. But we're not bringing everybody. And I'm thinking, 'You didn't think I knew that?' And his reply is: 'I knew that you knew it, but you're the one who likes to talk about degrees of intensity.'"

1　See glossary

Immediately after this communication, I received a visitation by not one, but two other Archangels: Uriel and Michael, in that order of appearance. I might have questioned the validity of that experience, except that Jack (a spiritual intuit in his own right who did not take ayahuasca) was in the room with me. Amazingly, he had the exact same experience, telling me who was present before I had the chance to tell him. The visuals (feelings) that were communicated to each of us were exactly the same. What then followed was a dialogue from Michael:

> "He's actually saying, as we're approaching this, that it empowers them. They are empowered more by Source. As we get closer to this He is saying, 'Surely you must know, all the dark forces know what is upon them.' He's saying that before this, 'These miscreants had to deal with us, we had to take (combative measures)' . . . describing like hand-to-hand combat. 'Before they had to deal with us, now they have to take on the Creator . . . and when this happens, rather than having to deal with all these demons, we're going to enjoy the supreme position of being spectators. And we just can't wait' . . . Their mood is celebratory."

At that point I continued to comment in the third person on what I was observing.

> "They are in awe of what's going on. They are saying that there are things that the Creator does that are even mysterious to us. 'Simply because we're Archangels doesn't mean we know all things. And so even unto us, there are mysteries.' And there will be . . . apparently what God's doing will even affect the angelic realm in terms of the expansiveness of their knowledge and understanding. This is really unbelievable.

> "It's not like this just happens to humanity and the rest of Creation is untouched. It affects everyone. All of Creation: on all levels, on all planes, in all parallel universes. (However) unlike us, they don't have to prepare. They're so close to God. They're waiting for it, but they don't have to prepare. And their vibration is such that . . . understand that as it is in this moment . . . our potential is beyond theirs, but at this moment they are so far above us, their vibration is so (much higher than ours) . . . I'm experiencing it now. Understand that Archangels are extremely rare and powerful creatures . . . and they are with God. They hardly need to prepare. The kind of

communications I've been having with God, the Archangels have (that) in every moment. You can't even refer to time-space with them as you do with us. They are constantly with God, doing God's Will. (They) enjoy the flow of being in attune with God's Will. So . . . they hardly need to prepare. But even unto them there are mysteries to 2012 that they will not know until God finally decides 'it's time to party.'"

The next part of the communication seemed to make a reference to my work with the Creator, and it came obliquely after Jack asked about Divine protection:

"He's saying that Source will provide all the answers we need. Understand something right now; they're kind of like almost . . . how do I explain this? . . . Hold on a moment (now speaking in the vernacular to emphasize the point) 'We don't entirely understand it, but if that's what the Boss wants, it's fine with us.' That's kind of a rough (translation) . . . it's more like, 'We don't fully understand it, but if it's what the Boss wants . . . it has to be important, or the Boss wouldn't have done this.' They actually don't understand why . . . they don't even understand why I was chosen for this. They have this wait-and-see attitude about what's going to happen at the end of this year, as well. It's mysterious to me (too), because they're so close to God . . . and they're in constant joy. Fulfilling God's Will is the source of their bliss . . . it's where their power and their bliss come from. And they're so close to God . . . but even unto them there are mysteries."

"And I'm getting the distinct impression that whatever transpires tonight, they are staying with us because I'm getting the sense they are among many others. They want to observe, I guess. [Jack: "I know."] And the most bizarre part is that I'm picking up that they were here in previous sessions, but now they are showing great interest. Also . . . something that seems strange . . . this is a paradox to me, I don't know how this works, they do each have distinctive personalities. They're not robots. Each one of them is extremely powerful in their own right . . . they have free will. But they have aligned themselves with the will of God because there is such joy and fulfillment in doing God's will. Even though they have free will, they would never, for a moment, do something that is contrary to God's will, contrary to what God wanted . . ." [Jack:

"I knew already this."]

"I asked them who else was present with us. They almost communicate with me in 'one-mindedness.' Michael is not speaking to me as an individual. Michael is speaking to me as (all) three. They have the ability to communicate as one consciousness. They don't have to, but sometimes they chose to. I asked who else is present, and they told me, 'You have no idea.' So I guess on the angelic realms there is like a huge audience for this . . . (long pause) . . . I asked them if the evil forces know this is going on and they said, 'Yes,' and I said, 'That's not making me feel very good.' And they said, 'They've got something much bigger than you to worry about right now.' And I asked, 'What is that?' And they replied, 'Converts.' *[Jack: "Converts?"]* There are some demonic forces that are jumping ship and coming to the side of good and that's . . . they're telling me that that's the preoccupation of the dark forces right now. That they're losing numbers . . . and this conversion, it has an accelerated quality to it. I'm getting the sense (it's) just the last couple of months. This has not been going on for a long time."

"And they're telling me it's going to get worse for them. They are saying that that particular phenomenon would have happened whether I was in the picture or not. That was already in the cards. It's completely divorced from anything that you and I are doing . . . they are showing me these vast demonic realms. Just as there are vast realms of beings on the angelic realms, there are also vast realms on the dark side. There are universes of creatures, both on the good side and on the dark side. What they're telling me is, the dark forces are intelligent. They have access to pretty much the same information that we do . . . There are dark forces that are aware of these communications. God won't stop it. And there are dark forces that are observing our communications that have been so affected by it. Their hearts are changing. There are dark forces that realize that this is a losing battle. They're not stupid. And so — in the deeper realms of darkness, this is scary. The dark forces are frightened by this. *[Jack: "Because they've never had to fight directly against Source."]* Yes. And as far as Michael and (the archangels go) . . . they are almost giddy over it. They have been fighting the good fight for so

long, that they are giddy over it. *[Jack: (Jokingly) 'My Daddy's gonna getcha.']* **Yeah, that's the (gist of it)."**

For the next few minutes, I held a discourse with Jack and Cathryn, wherein they asked different questions, and I would respond from my altered state. For instance, Cathryn asked about the contents of the third revelation from Fatima, which the Catholic Church has refused to release to the public. The essence of the reply was that there were certain comments in the third revelation that implicated Church fathers in their cooperation with dark forces — something too embarrassing for those in authority to ever allow a public disclosure.

Suddenly and unexpectedly, I interrupted the dialogue.

"I'm being administered to at the moment, please . . . I'm being shown what's wrong with me . . . What they're saying is that this has to be done first before it can go to the next level. *[Cathryn: "It's okay, we're here."]* **The sense I'm getting is that this is a pretty big jump, so they're having to work on me, to ready me . . ."**

What followed was a meeting between me and my "inner child"— who looked so bloodied, scarred, and beat up as to appear severely deformed. The appearance of a small boy, no more than four years old — that was me, looking so brutalized that he appeared to be barely holding onto life, was more than I could take. I began crying so uncontrollably that my recorded comments became undecipherable.

"I knew I had to hang on," said the small boy, **"because I knew what you had to do. You've known it all along, too. It was only in your conscious mind that you forgot, because you had to keep functioning in the real world."**

Translating a thought that was echoing from the angelic realm, I said, "On a subconscious level, we all know our mission."

At this point Cathryn and Jack were speaking aloud, trying to console me. However, this only proved to be a source of irritation because all thoughts around me (earthly and heavenly) were being amplified to the point where it became more than I could process. On all psychic levels, I was on overload.

"Aside from me telling you all these things I am utterly in awe. The sight of Archangels is just . . . and then, what I'm going through now. Any attempt to describe it borders on mockery. I don't know. Words cannot describe the profoundness of it all

. . . (and now) they're working on me."

When we began this session, we had hoped to get more valuable revelations that evening to help "fill the gaps" in the development of this book, but the Divine had other things in Mind. It soon became apparent that this would be a "healing session," as I could feel the presence of untold legions of angelic beings. Several hundred of them were "around me," constantly attending to me, producing this irritating feeling that I was being primped. Still crying, I blurted aloud in frustration, **"They're kinda making me feel like a** *prima donna*. **This is ridiculous. Queen bee . . . with all these worker bees around you. You're the center of attention** . . . (and then in response to their reassurances) . . . **Yeah, yeah, yeah, (sure) . . . like I'll feel so much better when this is over."**

What followed this was my introduction to thousands upon thousands of my previous lives as a human soul. The pain and anguish I experienced was so great that the resulting recording of the event contains lamentations that are barely recognizable, interrupted by long stretches of violent, audible weeping.

At a couple junctures during the session I cry out to my wife, **"Oh my God . . . it feels like they're operating on me without anesthetics! This is so painful!"** Beyond that, there are outbursts that contain a pleading to Jack and Cathryn not to say anything more, to comments about my experience of my other selves, to comments about language: **"Facets of so many previous incarnations, there are just no words . . . NO WORDS! It's such a big deal! The whole universe is in on it! . . . Oh my God! Thoughts are being amplified. It's so irritating. I can see the whole thing. A thought arises in your brain, and then the part of your brain that uses language, and then . . . I'm sorry. It's irritating. The way we use language to communicate when we could just give each other the totality of our thought! Oh my God. Language** (how limiting!) . . . **Plato was right!"**

And then moments later: **"I can't deal with this spectacle. It's just overwhelming. There are so many around me . . . 'Why are you all around me?' . . . I have hundreds of personal assistants. I don't know what's going on! I don't know if they can put me back together . . ."**

Many of the comments that followed are directed to Cathryn, because in the latter half of the session I felt like such a completely different person. In my state of crisis, despite being in a very strong marriage, I actually wondered if she would still want to remain married to me. **"The things that are going on tonight (are) reverberating to the very edges of our universe. It is so important . . . that I'm having trouble internalizing it, because I don't know what internal is! I'm experiencing being multiple** people from my past — at the same time. And I'm conscious of each of these different levels simultaneously and it's overwhelming. It's so unreal." *[Cathryn: "And Source told you to get used to it?"]* "Yes . . . I had so many abilities that I don't have now, that I need to finish my mission. Thousands of personalities that I've been throughout the universe that I didn't know about! I'm so sorry I'm putting you through this." *[Cathryn: "It's okay."]*

The experience of Creation as a unified whole while still in a fragmented state only appeared to worsen my short-term state of crisis: "It's so fragmented, I'm trying to process it . . . I'm having problems determining (the difference between) subject and object. It gets down to some very basic ideas. Oh, Cathryn, I'm seeing my whole circuitry. I mean . . . *[Cathryn: "It must be fascinating."]* I have been in preparation for this for many lifetimes. And He's showing me that . . . Who am I? . . . I can't even cry (now), because to cry I have to have an 'I'."

And then moments later I utter a series of statements that appear only later to be so disjointed as to be incomprehensible:

"I have been so many people. I am so old (an old soul) . . . and the reason I'm being told we didn't have these abilities is because our third dimension is so dense. Even now, there's a battle going on . . . I'm sorry, Cathryn, but this is so painful. He is orchestrating it! . . . . God did the whole thing. He's saying, 'It's okay . . . .' I'm getting all this love and support . . . even with all this support, it's just so painful. I'm going through some kind of metamorphosis . . . . the things I've seen. Cathryn, I wish I could share this with you, and I'm so sorry that you can't (share it with me) . . . We've been preparing for this for so long. I'm crying because you can't see this and you deserve to be able to see it . . ."

A short time later, after an extended period of silence, I turned to my wife, with eyes still closed, speaking slowly and softly in her direction:

"Do you want to know what enlightenment is? *[Cathryn: "Yes. What is it?"]* "It is the peeling away of an unbelievable number of different levels of your self. Like an onion many times over. It's going through the process of peeling away. So you come to the conclusion that you must be (one with) God. Because He created you and . . . you come to the conclusion that it's all One and the Same! . . . When this is all over, you'll have to go through the same thing. Because enlightenment is about not hanging on to anything. It's just about . . . *[Cathryn: ". . . returning to Source."]* . . . Give it a little bit of time and the experience will become commonplace. COMMONPLACE!

"I'm able to experience Greg Caton as a separate (entity). I always had the ability to experience Greg Caton as something separate. . ."

Rather than feeling transformed, I felt more disoriented than in any previous session:

"Everything is third person and it's so bizarre. Oh God . . . all these angelic beings . . . There are all these layers about what Greg Caton is . . . Cathryn, either I'm completely psychotic, or I'm being transformed . . . . Because God made the decision . . . it's like God couldn't continue this until I got healed, partly because I didn't have the equipment. Cathryn, you have no idea the wounds I've been carrying – the injuries I've been carrying . . . *[Cathryn: "It is apparent from your outer personality that you are wounded."]* It is only by the Grace of God . . . because there is no physician in any of the realms that could possibly heal someone who (has incurred) this many wounds – this many hurts for countless lifetimes. *[Cathryn: "I wish I could get . . ."]* You will (be healed). I felt (your) thought . . . You will. God knows that. He knows everything. He knows the pain that you're in. He knows . . . He is telling me just be patient . . ."

This leads to a very personal experience where I was able to experience my wife on a soul level as I re-directed my focus:

"You are more precious to me than you were before, because I've seen your soul now. You are very precious to God. You are precious to Him. You're such a good person. You don't know. You're like me. When we came down here we were just like sheep lead to the slaughter. We're too innocent. We just don't understand a world that's full of evil people. We just don't understand it. It doesn't make any sense. Through your whole life, things have seemed a little out of place, because they're so messed up!"

The dialogue that followed only showed more demonstrably the state of extreme confusion I was in, as I addressed my lamentation to Source itself:

"'How could YOU do this? God, how could you create this mess? You're not supposed to do stuff like this!' And He's saying you won't understand it all until the end. 'Why do I have to wait 'til the end?!' . . . (long pause) . . . I don't know what your experience of this is or what you think of me now!" [*Cathryn: "I think this is a miracle that you're able to go through this."*]

The dialogue that followed further enunciated my crisis with my own identity, as I alternated between talking to the Divine and talking to my wife:

"I need to get my 'am' back. My identity . . . Once you lose your identity, then that's when you see the Infinite. Because to see the Infinite, you yourself must be Infinite." [*Cathryn: "OK."*] And then, after a long pause: "I've been here for so long. Most people who talk about being 'born again' have no idea what it means to be 'born again.' It's about losing your identity, and I only have to learn how to control this, because this is going to look very weird. You'll feel all this love from me to you, Cathryn, because I see all these things that I didn't see before. It's hard for me as your husband because I'm having to deal with what is the 'am' that loves you? And the conclusion I'm left with is that it's your own self-reflection. It's the Infinite. It's the Divine Loving you back. And you, in particular, have a very special soul . . ."

Shortly after this, the session was over, the single most profound journey I had ever taken in my life. Nonetheless, so profound was the experience, so other-worldly, that still, there existed room for doubt in my normal state of awareness. I had had a transformative experience, but the transformation was not complete. There were other questions I had concerning this experience with which I was wrestling. Whereas my other experiences of higher states of consciousness were marked by extreme bliss, this was the most painful emotional journey to date — and I wasn't the only one to notice it.

Only in the aftermath of listening to the recording of this event three days later did I realize that my wife was having problems witnessing the paradox of what appeared to be a spiritual awakening with the most contrary spectacle of a husband in extreme pain.

At one point in the session, she asks pleadingly, "Is there any joy in the . . .?"

"NO! Not right now!" I cry out loudly, interrupting her, and then returning to sobs.

"It's like you didn't experience any joy!" she responds sadly.

In the days that followed this experience, I also had problems processing my experience with the Archangels and the experience turned out to be quite hurtful.

"The Archangels really don't understand," I told Cathryn one morning, mournfully.

"What do you mean?" she replied.

"They told me that even though they work right next to the Creator, and serving Him is the source of their joy and their bliss, that there are still mysteries that are beyond them. There are still elements of the Divine Will that are beyond their ability to comprehend."

"Why is this a problem for you?" Cathryn pressed.

"Because deep within the many layers of this single thought transmission I could tell that my own relationship with the Creator was puzzling them."

"Which means what?"

"Okay, let me spell it out for you in the vernacular. Although it was no one's intention to hurt or insult, I could tell that the Archangels were mystified that I would be doing this kind of work. In other words, it's as if they had harbored the thought, 'Of all the people that God could have chosen, is it really possible that He couldn't do any better than this bum? Aren't there spiritual adepts out there who would have been a better fit? But what the heck . . . if this is what the Boss wants, it's fine with us!' I know they didn't mean to convey this, but it's what I picked up. And because these angels are so pure and so magnificent and so close to God and it is such an incredible honor to be in their presence, you have to know that I feel just crushed over this. I mean . . . it really, really hurt my feelings. And I'm having to deal with this, while at the same time I'm still processing everything else I had to endure from the other night. I told the Divine in the very beginning that I didn't feel worthy of this. I told Him that I didn't want the job. After everything that's happened, I still feel lost."

In the days that followed I found myself even more disoriented, to the point where I didn't take another journey until April 21st. But as more information was revealed, I better understood the importance of this 'preparatory session' and was grateful.

"Do you see O my brothers and sisters?
It is not chaos or death—it is form, union, plan—it
is eternal life — it is Happiness."

~ Walt Whitman — "Song of Myself"

Chapter 6:

Mysteries of the Singularity

"God is withdrawing his support (for the dark forces). 'You're on your own now. . .' the feeling of it . . . no words. He is withdrawing, and when He does they'll be left with nothing. I was allowed to feel Him withdrawing His Essence, His Force . . . And what He says now is, 'They're on their own. If they're willing to continue the delusion that they were anything separate from Me, let them continue . . . without (My) support.'"

Beginning in April, my ayahuasca journeys became increasingly thematic, with more attention being given to key elements of the Passage. One session, held on a Saturday evening (April 21), was particularly devoted to conditions surrounding the Singularity. However, we found that stretching our inquiry to the far edges of man's ability to comprehend has its risks. Some of the revelations brought increased clarity, while others made the mystery of the event even more glaring.

"The whole idea that God is dead or that He didn't take an interest in His Creation is totally wrong. He has a very, very active role in everything in Creation. He does. We just don't see it, but He does. The great mystery is no matter how contrary to God it seems, everything that's happened had a purpose. There is this immense sense of Wholeness and Connectedness. And now, it is all collapsing to a point . . . They (the dark forces) are already aware that the collapse has begun. So now we're being narrowed down this passageway that will take us to the Great Singularity."

Drawing upon revelations from a previous reading, Jack made the following query, wherein the response, at first, seems like a complete non-sequitur:

["How can there be a Singularity if the New Earth and the Old Earth are separate?" asked Jack] **You're right. You're exactly** right. That's what (is) even more disastrous. He's showing this to me now . . . How can the souls (going to the Old Earth) come back? They're NOT part of the singularity! That's the whole point . . . How do these souls work their way back? . . . I don't understand . . . Think of a huge ball, and all of Creation and all of . . . everything in the multiverse is inside that ball. What I'm telling you is that the Devolved Earth is outside the singularity. *[Jack: "OK.. . ."]* It's clearly outside. *[Jack and Cathryn: "Already?"]* These people don't understand. It's a juncture so important that . . . it's a decision you have to make as to whether or not you're a part of the Singularity. *[Jack: "Is the Singularity returning Home to Source?"]* It's all part of the unfolding. It's hard to explain. Everything has been choreographed . . . to an extent you can't imagine. The whole thing is like a choreographed stage production. Everything has been choreographed, and on His level of consciousness, it all makes sense . . . and to the rest of us it's (completely) confusing. But in His Mind He's got everything figured out. Everything. Nothing has left His attention.

"I wish you could see what I'm seeing. You want to know why the world's getting crazy and more evil than ever? Because God is withdrawing His support — so they know they're having to (go to more outrageous means to get 'fed'). It's like when you deprive an animal of food, it will do things that it wouldn't have otherwise done if you hadn't left it hungry. So now they're hungry, so they're having to do more and more outrageous things, because they need to feed off our fear and our loathing and (our other negative emotions) . . . They're feeling starved so they're going through even more dramatic (antics), while at the same time attempting to co-opt the Singularity."

Later in the same session, I repeat Jack's question myself, because after channeling the message, I realized that, I too, was lost:

"He is saying, 'I have known about this since the beginning of Creation.' Everything was in His Mind. Everything, ultimately, is within the Mind of God. That's why this is a complete mystery (to me) ... How could there be this Old Earth outside the Singularity, if everything is within the Mind of God? And what He's saying is, 'Even until the end there are certain mysteries you won't understand until you share with Me the Mind of

God. Until you can come back into Me, and fold back into Me, you will never be able to understand. You cannot understand Godliness unless you're inside the Mind of God because outside any other framework, it doesn't make sense."

And later, the following message is received, which emphasizes that the act of Unity itself brings an end to mysteries and unanswered questions:

"It's like, in the Heart of God, He's aching for this, and He's waited so long. However, you, as a *seeker*, have wanted to reunite with Source. You can't imagine going back to Source Itself, which is the amplification of any emotion you could possibly think of that's good or pure. In His Heart . . . amplify that millions of times more. So if you could know (from his perspective) how much He wants you back, the intensity! Whatever love we have, it's just a drop from His Heart. So if you're in the middle of His Heart . . . it's this intensity, it's this intensity of joyousness, and it's really overwhelming. There's such a sense of Wholeness, and no one's really going to know what Wholeness is until they've been through this because we all have been in the dark for so long. You just can't begin to imagine it. But in Wholeness, everything is understood. There are no more questions . . . you just understand. You have this understanding."

In March of 2012 I received my first "instruction" that the journeys I had been taking were revealing information that should be incorporated into a book. With scarcely nine months to go until the "big event," the idea of producing such a book seemed like sheer insanity to me. With all my other responsibilities, I had no desire to publish anything; however, later that month, Jack intervened and offered to help. He felt the revelations of my sessions were too important not to find their way into print.

Despite the fact that publishing a book about 2012 with 45% of the year already behind us appeared sheer foolishness, I agreed. Jack flew to Ecuador on April 1st, and as you can see from previous chapters, he became an indispensable companion in journeys that followed. His next question in this session lead to more details about 'The Singularity': "Why is the book coming out now, so late in the game?"

"He is saying if it didn't come out late in the game, it wouldn't be in accordance with the Divine Plan. He's saying, 'I've orchestrated everything' and, as I've said before (going back to the Christmas metaphor) **certain things can't happen until 'Christmas time.' And in the consciousness of you and I, it makes no sense; but in the mind of the Divine, it does.** *[Jack: "And what happens to the children who are too young to understand the message?"]* **First of all, you are focusing on physical entities of a body, not taking into account where that soul is in other planes, on parallel universes — some of whose fragments are on the other side. So, He is saying you can't view . . . he doesn't view things in terms of children. He views things in terms of (where individuals are as) souls. This is all on the level of soul development.**

"So, He is communicating with souls directly . . . are you ready to come Home? And those souls who are ready to be part of unfolding into Singularity are coming Home, and those who don't (won't). I have to say this . . . it's beyond my comprehension. If it's about Singularity, how can something be outside the Singularity? I don't even understand that. That will have to be left as a big question mark. This is about a decision to be part of the Oneness, or not be part of the Oneness. And it may be a mystery to us on our level of consciousness, what would it mean to be outside the Singularity? Just like you asked earlier what the (splitting) earths looked like, the Singularity is bright and full of life and bigger, like you cannot believe. And I am telling you, on the dark side, there is not one shade of color.

"This feels more real than anything in the 'real' world. This feels like, this is it. As I've said before, as improbable as it may seem, this is it. This is return to Home . . . either you're in or you're out. I'm feeling a sense of finality to it all. This is it. This is where you get to see the *last act* **of the play. And after that, there are no more acts. This is the end of the play. This is an ending.**

[Jack: "So, no more incarnations?"] **"I won't say that, Jack. I can only tell you what I'm told. I am beyond speculating . . . in the mode I'm in right now, I tell you only what I receive. I give you nothing more. I don't exaggerate or embellish or put any of myself into it. I am telling you what I'm told. And if there isn't more, there isn't more. But there is this sense that there are all these edges that if we proceed beyond certain edges,**

there is no human being on this earth who can comprehend it. It is mysterious and it resides in the Mind of God. It is beyond the capabilities of humans to understand it. However, He says, that is about to change, because He wants us in His Mind. He wants us to see. He wants us to share with Him why things couldn't have been any other way."

Continuing the same inquiry, concerning the 'timing' of the book, the following was later received:

"**Stop worrying about the book . . . in His mind, this is on autopilot. You and I are still back here on earth, struggling and worrying (with) concerns and doubts and everything else, but in the mind of God, everything is complete . . .** [*Jack: "And unfolding."*] "**You can't keep a secret from God. It's not like you can really have a conspiracy or a revolt against God. That was an illusion. Because it all came from the One, and that's what these dark forces don't understand. It all emanates from the One. It never came from any place else.**"

Staying on the theme of the book, Jack asked about our ongoing "search for nexus points" for the section of this book that carries the same name:

"**He's saying these are important . . . He's actually giving me several reasons. There's almost an unfoldment of enlightenment in our act of doing it, because enlightenment is about seeing the Whole. And as we proceed along this path of digging up more nexus points, He is saying we will begin to see as we're doing it ... he's saying there's going to be a lot more we're going to add that we're not aware of. But He's saying that in the act of the *search* ... until we reach the Singularity, the search is still important. This whole book is about the search! This whole book is about trying to *inflame the passion of the heart* within people so that they realize that in the heart . . . *the heart is the portal*. Just like ayahuasca is a portal for me to communicate with the Divine, the *heart* is the portal through which people can experience the Love, and the Love only comes from one place, and that's God. That's why the heart is so important. No other chakra is as intimately connected with love as is the heart. That's why even in our lore, even in our romantic literature and everything else, (it is) the relationship between the heart and love (which is** the key). And I understand that's not in all cultures, (for in some cultures the role of the heart is not understood). But, nonetheless, in most cultures there is some unmistakable relationship between the heart and love. So no chakra is as intimately connected with love as is the heart.

"That's why the whole universe will be affected by this, because if you've got this little tiny point in space, (an infinitesimal point in space) and it's called planet Earth. And this infinitesimal point in space is the Heart Chakra of the Universe, if it's ill, that reverberates throughout the whole universe! Because it's the Universe's Heart Chakra. So the corruption and everything else that we've had is affecting — you just can't imagine — it goes so far beyond (Earth). And we can't grasp that. Because back in the relative mind, (we doubt). 'Many millions of light years we're talking, that's impossible.' It just can't happen. None of those things matter in the Mind of the Divine. They just don't. It's trivial nonsense. It's all part of the illusion, and NOW . . . what He's saying is that as this thing goes (forward), whatever it is we're doing, it's not occurring in a vacuum. It's not as if we are going to do something and nothing out there is happening. Because remember this really is about a collective Singularity that you're going to see. As the year proceeds, you're going to have more and more signs of the unfoldment because the unfoldment can't happen unless ultimately it totally engulfs the 3rd dimension. (In fact) it has to engulf ALL dimensions, right? [Jack: "Yes."] ... Or it wouldn't be the Singularity! So what He's saying is, whatever we're doing, understand that it's all part of this unfoldment."

Another recurring message throughout the sessions was that people should learn to 'feel' the message instead of trying to intellectualize it:

"This is from Source to you, Jack. He is giving you a feeling now of what everyone (who returns to Source) will be feeling. This huge, expansive universe (is) collapsing into the One. So you have to open your heart right now, to feel everything, everything, everything, all this fragmentation, folding back to where it came from. Back to the One who was the Source of all Creation from the very beginning. It's the collapse (of all fragmentation) into the One."

Though I was receiving the 'messages,' at times even I was surprised that Source would answer certain questions so obliquely, and at other times, not at all. This was particularly true when questions were raised that addressed small, trivial matters. During the April 21st session, I became quite ill, but still I continued to push forward with the session. Out of concern, Jack asked if I could be given a 'healing' so that I could more comfortably continue. But the Divine wasn't about to go in a different direction or go 'off-message':

" . . . You're in the muck now and He has compassion for you. There is nothing that you're going through that He doesn't understand, but if you could see it from His perspective, the third dimension *is an illusion*. It's a complete illusion. And what He's dealing with is the reality (of) it all. So if we speak or we think or we feel in the language of illusion, our answers will be illusionary. We have to think in terms of (the Singularity). He understand this is not real (to us) because we're not there yet, so this is going to sound like a paradox, even unto itself. That to get the answers to some of the things you want to ask, you'd have to be able to step outside the boundaries of the illusionary language, and think in terms of the Singularity. And He understands that this is almost impossible, but again, be patient. I know you're not going to understand this — forgive me for saying this — but He is so proud of Himself. (This has the feel of) a little kid who's ready to pee in his pants, because He's so excited. Okay? It's like He can't contain Himself . . . He's been preparing for this for such a long time . . . and now ayahuasca is showing me all the champagne glasses again (okay, I get it!). There are so many beings in the higher realms that are giddy with excitement. Just as there are those who want to continue to (fool around and) play character."

And again, in response to another trivial question:

" . . . if it's in the Plan, it's got a reason, even if this is a mystery to us. Except one thing, which He is saying will never be a mystery to us and was out in the open all along, and that is, 'That you have left Me, but eventually, you must return to Me, because this is your Home.' We have all known on some level through all our incarnations that eventually, it was the Destiny of all of us, that it would come to this. This return back into the One. It's an immense thing. I know that my words are completely inadequate to express this. I, of all people, know how limited language is and it's many deficiencies, but if you would feel what I feel and experience, it is the collapse back into the One and that is where our fulfillment and our bliss and our sense of completion (reside), so complete that we can't possibly (understand). It's a cup that is so full you can't possibly put anything else into it. Fullness of Joy. Fullness of Bliss. Fullness of Absolute Love. It is a feeling of such total completion (so) that never would the thought enter the mind of the Soul that it needs anything else. It is complete, as we cannot now understand complete. It is total Wholeness in every respect."

An analogy followed:

"If you take a glass, and you throw it on the floor and it shatters into a thousand pieces, each piece still owes its home to that glass. And you can pretend that those shards of glass on the floor came from somewhere else, and you pretend all you want to . . . but we are all shards of glass (in the same way). When Creation happened *(swoosh — making a sound imitating the 'going out')* in a process that takes billions of years, (having emanated from the Divine) each of those shards of glass have to come back. (Now) it's like time going in reverse. All the shards must return to the glass because that's where they came from. They don't belong to anything else."

At this point Jack attempted to fit the coming Singularity into the traditional Eastern concept of the four cyclic "yugas" — since the creation of the New Earth was compared to the onset of a Sat Yuga, which, at this time, would be outside the normally accepted cycle.

"This transcends (the cycles of) yugas[1]. (He's) telling me about this New Earth . . . the New Earth is inside the Mind of God. The Whole! If you have the awareness that It's all Him, then you realize that you'll never, at that point, confuse actor from character. And you'll know that in that Earth, it is all about experiencing His Love and His Bliss, in a different way. But it's still within the One . . . *[Jack: "What does Love have to do with the Singularity?"]* "They are One and the Same . . . The Singularity is the Love. And the Love is the Singularity. And He's saying that from whatever perspective you're looking

---

1   See Wikipedia — (http://en.wikipedia.org/wiki/Yugas)

at, all forms of Love, however twisted they may be, however disjointed and screwed up they may be — they were all, in fact, a hidden form of yearning to find the thing they didn't know they were looking for . . . which was the One, no matter what kind of perversion you can think of. It's an extreme twisting of the yearning (to return Home) . . . but still the Source of all of that ... the source of every sexual perversion is a twisted form of the yearning to be part of the One . . . the yearning to be part of where you came from! *[Jack: "It's part of the Great Separation".]* Yes ... so you have this Bliss when you were part of the (One) in God's Mind. So now you're in Creation and you no longer have that Bliss, so it's like through all our incarnations, we've been trying to get back to where we came from. We're trying to get back to the Bliss."

"In your hearts you've all known, through all your incarnations; that this is what it comes to — the Conclusion. And the only thing you're having difficulty with is the relative mind believing it couldn't possible be *now.* And what He's saying is, 'It IS now.' What is about to happen is something which at some level each soul knows that this is where it goes. This is the destiny of every Soul, because, again, this is where you came from! And the only thing that's going to confuse us is our concept of Time, which doesn't exist in God's Mind (anyway). Time is something that we created. God didn't create Time. We did. So, He's saying . . . that you have all known, from the Beginning, through countless incarnations — you've all known about this Event, secretly, in your hearts. Certainly the experience, is beyond any detail you can possibly communicate. You have to wait for Christmas!"

Cathryn asked about the three days of darkness, if its purpose was "to get to the other side," and surprisingly, Source responded almost as if it were an after-thought:

"He's (already) described this as an astrophysical event. I'm getting now that certain things are happening that's almost for our (benefit). It's as if WE need it. In His mind, if the center of the Milky Way (Galaxy) was to evaporate tomorrow, He would still (proceed) on schedule. No matter what happens, the show must go on. I'm sorry. I can't find any other way to explain it."

At this point in the session I was so overwhelmed by the substance of the communications, the emotions that were flowing through me, and the improbability of everything that had been expressed as my "relativistic mind" interpreted it, that I began to break down. I was very weak, faint, and exhausted from vomiting:

"I'm so sorry, Jack, if ever I express doubts to you, it's only because this is just so overwhelming. Again, I'm just giving you the verbal translation of what's been communicated to me. It's just so overwhelming and I'm just ... I can't imagine there being a soul out there that is sick enough to make (all) this up. It doesn't seem like it would come from anywhere else (but God). But it is this Infinite Authority that's just so overwhelming. It doesn't have the characteristics of personality. Angels, I've got them. Archangels, I've got them. Negative forces, I've got them. Raksasas, demons, elementals, humans on the other side ... I can tell what they are by their vibration. But this, this is beyond everything ... If this isn't Source, what else could it be?

[Jack: "Asks directly. Is this coming from Source?"] "He is saying, 'I reverberate my 'AM-ness' to every heart in the universe. I reverberate my Oneness, my AM-ness, My Self in my myriad, myriad forms, throughout Creation.'"

As the session proceeded I experienced a state of such intense Unity that I perceived the energy of the query and the energy of the response as being one and the same. Rather than being a joyful experience, I found it irritating and confusing:

[Jack: "I ask Source to speak through you directly, giving Source permission to speak directly through you ... to step aside, so that a direct message, in Source's words ..."] "Jack, with all due respect, if you could be on my side and not your side (of the experience) . . . you don't understand. He hears every question you ask before you ask it. You'd have to see it from where I'm standing. It's like God talking to Himself. So know . . . know, Jack . . . that if it's God talking to Himself, He's got it all figured out before it ever comes out of your mouth. He understands the compassion, the compassion in which you asked the question, in which you made the request, and this is the only way I can convey this to you. He's saying, 'Have faith. I have it covered.' It's the only way I can think of

to describe, 'Have faith. I've got it covered.' I know that leaves people like you and I dissatisfied, but that's the message."

Jack found this response less than satisfying. He became more insistent that I strengthen my connection to get a "word-for-word" download of what it was that God had to communicate. This was the response:

"No, you're misunderstanding me. He's saying that to communicate in the third dimension, He still needs to have someone . . . there still has to be an antenna out there that can take His Vibration and translate it into language. Does that make any sense? So, I'm this antenna . . . and maybe this should be emphasized in the introduction. Any imperfection in this text is entirely mine. But I am getting this overwhelming sense that He is pleased with how things are going. He seems very (pleased) . . . remember, (this) is what frustrates you. He's not giving me words. He doesn't lower Himself to that. He gives thought impressions and I have to try with everything that is in me to faithfully communicate those thought impressions to words. It's a step down in vibration. You have to know that. You can't take something as full as Wholeness, and chop it up and turn into words and not lose something. That isn't possible. You can't take Wholeness and chop it into words and still have the same force and effect. We can TRY, but it isn't the real (original) thing. Feeling love and reading about it is not the same thing. The feeling of love is so much more powerful than if you just read about it — if they were just words."

In response to Cathryn's next question, "What (else) would Source want to be written in the book?" came the following response:

"You're trying too hard. Get into the flow. Just feel where this is going. Just feel the rightness of this. Is there any other direction that things could go right now in this moment? (Is there) any other message you could possibly conceive of in your mind that gives you more fulfillment, when you think about where this is going? Is there any message that could possibly be more Full than this one? And He's saying, 'No.' Because He's saying, as I said earlier, there can only be ONE message going into the Singularity. Or it wouldn't be the Singularity. What He's saying, as . . . once again, as I've said so many numerous times, this message is what we've been tasked with, and that's what we're doing. And I'll tell you something else. All of this struggling and worrying and everything else . . . (Cathryn, I know we're both exhausted, back in the relative world) but on His level of consciousness, there is none (*i.e. fatigue*). It's all . . . there's nothing but Fullness and Completion. And what He's saying is, this should be the focus: on the Return to where we all came from. The Return to Source.

"I'm having problems integrating. You know when this is (and isn't) from Source, so you don't have to remind me. But I give you these little footnotes so that you would know as a speaker, my perspective, because I think you should have both (my comments as distinct from the Divine's). We are still in the relative, so you should have both. Maybe it's more of a form of confirmation . . . so 'I know when Greg is talking and I know when it's Source.' You can feel the difference in vibration and He's encouraging that. Because that's what this exercise is about anyway. Ask yourself, 'Is this the Truth?' Ask yourself. Right along, isn't that what we're telling our readers to do? Well, we have to do the same thing. If this is not just for us to be talking to other people, to get them to listen; we should be listeners, too, to the very same message that we are learning to impart to others. It's all about listening on the level of heart. You'll know it all, if you listen on the level of heart. As it pertains to 2012, to even the broader question of where we're going as a people . . . what do we do with this growing unhappiness in the world? He's saying, there is a fulfillment connected with Truth. Truth has its own gratification. It has its own sense of fulfillment. And if you're proceeding to That, you know it has a charm that could only descend from the Divine. Then people will find no greater sense of fulfillment than what's in this Message. That's it. Beyond a certain point, the words don't matter. You either get it or you don't. I don't know — it's like . . . IT! This is it. And He's saying we've known it all along. We just didn't know when the party was going to start."

Cathryn then asked if we could get an exact date as to when the Passage would begin. The response:

"There is something to this Biblical expression, 'No one

knows when that day or hour will come . . . not the angels in heaven, not the Son, but only the Father.' There is something to keeping certain things a mystery. For being the Divine, He has a way of finding the most commonplace analogies, and He's even aware of it. He even has this incredible awareness of the feelings of a girl who is getting ready to go the prom. And she doesn't want to see the boy — she's got her make-up and her orchid or whatever — until she's completely ready. She doesn't want anybody to see her. She'd be embarrassed. She wants to be complete before she meets her date at the door and (then) they go off to the prom. And what is being conveyed to me is that this is a manifestation of the archetype. You have to understand the archetype. You have to understand what's going on here. We're returning to the Christmas metaphor — it all unfolds and have the faith that it will all be disclosed. You wouldn't be in Wholeness if you still had remaining questions, and He wouldn't be in Wholeness if there were still mysteries. You must open your heart and allow your mind to be God's Mind."

In a future discussion on the nature of Unity, I found it curious that for the second time in the session, Source would make a reference to sex:

"In a highly, highly diluted form, this is what sex is (unity). You want to feel a sense of Unity. But it's a very, very, very diluted version — and He made it that way, deliberately for the purpose of pro-creation. But the ultimate sex (act) is to be one with God. It's the ultimate sense of Wholeness and Fulfillment. All of these other perversions are just diluted (forms of) way down the line. So, the ultimate sex, the ultimate sense of Unity and Wholeness and (the feeling of) 'I feel fulfilled!' is that return to Source, because nothing could be more fulfilling than to return. There can be no greater Home, there can be no greater sense of 'I'm home!' than if you were to go back to where you originally came from. None of this will make any sense unless you can feel what is (transpiring) in this moment. It's in the feeling — the feeling, because the words will not convey it. And even in what we're doing — and of course, we're writing a book and it's full of words — is we're attempting to 'ping'. The words are just these things that try to 'ping' the heart. It's like, what we're telling people to do is WAKE UP! Wake up! You've been asleep for a VERY, LONG TIME! Now, wake up!"

Jack asks the following questions:

[Jack: *"There are many messages about 2012 and there's probably been more books about 2012 than any other year, ever . . ."*] **"And He is saying, 'I'm aware of ALL of them."** [*"And many say that all of what is to come will start in December, and it'll take 7 years to unfold, or whatever."*] **"No."** [*"That's not what you've told us."*] **"No."** [*"So ... what they've learned is wrong."*] **"Not only are they wrong, but you have to understand that the dark forces are going to have to pull every play in the book. As I've said this before, there are entities that will not survive this. They're not like we are. They're not immortals. So you have to understand as this thing reaches closer to Singularity . . . it's like Judy Garland showing the water on the Wicked Witch. 'I'm melting, I'm melting.' It's that same kind of desperateness. 'I'm melting!' They're desperate. And you can even feel that in this moment. 'I'm feeling the desperateness. How dare you do this! I've been what I am for millions of years! How dare you think of taking away my domain! THIS IS MINE! I OWN IT!' That's what evil is. 'This is mine! I own it! I'm the ultimate contrarian!' It would be naïve to think that you're going to take that away (without a fight)."**

"We've known what evil is all along, so why should we expect less? What He's saying is — even then He has compassion, but unless they are willing to stop and say (again), 'I'm an actor. This is a paycheck. It's time to clock out and go home to the wife and kids.' Unless people can get the difference between actor and character, they will not unite with the Singularity because the character was just a tool to get BACK to the Divine. That's why it's important to dissociate from your character. (Because) what He is saying is that 'I am collapsing the tools I used to get to this point.'

"It was like a literary device, it was a means to an end that wouldn't have happened (otherwise). We wouldn't have gotten to this point without it, but now it's outlived its usefulness. Okay? And because it's outlived its usefulness, however (the soul fragments) collapse into themselves, if the souls collectively, (and) if the souls in their unified form, make the decision to invest in unreality, then the end point (in terms of) where it goes is UNREALITY! Because there's only One. There's only reality inside the One. There is no reality outside the One."

At this point I enunciated the concept with a personal comment to my wife:

"This reminds me of Brahmananda Saraswati, the spiritual leader of the Jyotir Math in India.[2] He was the Shankaracharya, which is a very, high position within the Vedic community. The position this man held came from a religious figure in the eighth century, called Shankara. And in the twelfth century this Hindu polytheist was critical of Shankara, saying, 'The reason Shankara talked about the One is probably because he was so stupid he couldn't count any higher than one!' And what God is saying is, 'Not to de-legitimatize all the manifestations of the One (because) it's all a matter of what consciousness you're in.' At a certain level all these things are true (observations and cognitions on the various forms of God). The different gods and their vibrations, they all exist, but, do you want to stay there, or do you want to go to the very highest vibration (of all)? Where do you want to reside? At its highest level, there can be only One! And what He's saying is, you can take your hand, and you can point your (index) finger, or make a fist; you have all kinds of different forms (that) you can make with your hand. But at its essence, its very essence, is HAND-ness. That's its essence. It's a hand. And everything else is just an illusion. If I make a threatening gesture to you and you see a fist — however concrete that reality looks, as soon as I open my hand, that reality's been destroyed. That thing that you held as so concrete is now gone. Now, where's your reality? What He's saying is that those who invest in the CHARACTER are making the same mistake. They think the fist is real. 'If in My Divine Will, I open My Hand, what will happen to your reality?'"

Jack next asked a question about the permanence of the Singularity:

[Jack: "For those who go to the New Earth . . . will it be permanent or not? Will it last 1,000 years? Forever? What? I feel that I already know the answer, but I need to hear it."] "It's permanent. Because to revert (back to relativity), you have to

2   See Wikipedia (http://en.wikipedia.org/wiki/Brahmananda_Saraswati)

step out of the **Singularity**." *["And that's the cycle . . . there's no more cycles. There's just one . . ."]* **"Yes."** *["Understood."]* "So this really is a mass awakening for those who say, 'I want to be awakened. I want to get out of this mess.' As we proceed through the rest of this year, there is this Grace. God is going to do something for us He's never done before. We've been through lifetimes where we've asked God, 'Can you just give me a helping hand? Can you just help me out a LITTLE bit? I'm asking for help and I don't feel like I'm getting any!' And, of course, He feels all of that, and what I'm being told is, there is a special Grace, in a very real sense, He is throwing us a lifeline. So, it feels like He wants us back so bad, He's willing to do things right now He's never done before. And yet at the same time, it's the mystery. The mystery! He knew this from the beginning. I am (of course) explaining it in linear terms, so I know that it sounds like, 'Okay, God just finally made this decision.' Forget that . . . God doesn't make decisions. There's no time line with Him! How can God make a decision when the act of making a decision involves a time line! And God doesn't have one. The paradox is, we search for Truth and now we finally *find* Truth, and then we find that we can't understand our new Truth if we think with our linear, relativistic, dualistic mind. That's the paradox of it all. Everything makes sense inside the Mind of God. Nothing makes any sense anywhere else.

"If you want to understand a thought, and its meaning and its purpose, you have to go back to where it came from. Nothing in this universe makes (any) sense, unless it can be thought of in terms of where it came from. And since we all originated from the Singularity, nothing will make more sense than that.

"Do you remember when you were in the 5th grade? Do you remember 'set theory'? There's sets, and there's the intersection set. You had Set A, Set B — do you remember that, those exercises in grade school? And what He's saying is, what you and I are doing, is the Ultimate Set from which there are no subsets. This is *the Set*, and within itself EVERY-THING intersects. Again, words do not do justice to what's communicated to me here. The medium in which I'm working (with words) automatically makes me an imperfect communicator. But I'm doing my best, to take something that is so Divine, and have it make sense in such a way that it will ping the hearts of those who will only listen."

"As to the question of permanence, within the Singularity itself, there is only Reality and Non-Reality, so, again, you're either going to accept that the Hand is the Hand, God is God, Source is Source, Oneness is Oneness — there can be only one Ultimate Whole. You either believe in this, or you believe that the Fist has its own reality, which we know it does not. He's saying, if you identify with unreality, and that's where you invest your self, you're cut from the Source of what you are . . . This whole idea that you could have this other (devolved) Earth and it's not within the Singularity, makes no sense at all to me. But I've gotten a re-affirmation tonight of this Split, and as I view it, it is very real. I understand now, in this moment, in terms of archetype, where the Judeo-Christian-Islam *(i.e. Abrahamic religious)* concept comes from, not to mention all the other religions that prescribe to this, that there is this HELL *that lasts forever*. I have to be honest. I don't think until this moment that I really believed that such a thing could exist. And now I do because, if you invest of yourself in unreality, that unreality is unreal. It's unreal 5 minutes from now. It's unreal a million years from now. And if you give it a billion years, (it will make no difference). You cannot take something that is unreal and turn it, *magically*, into something that is Real, (with nothing) but the mere passage of time. It doesn't work. That is where the concept of *everlasting hell* comes from. It is permanent disconnection from God, because you used the full weight of your volition to say, 'I don't need you. Or I don't want you. I am not part of You.' And you are using your volition to identify yourself with (a mere) character. How you would reconcile this with the idea that one may merely cycle for 20,000 or 30,000 more lives, I am not sure."

In connection with the writing of this book, the Divine commented on the importance of following through with one's purpose, one's mission or dharma:

"The act of fulfilling our mission is a part of the unfoldment for us personally. It came out of this huge, vast void of Love and Joy, and we're going to go back to it. And it's going to feel like — we're back in the womb. We're going to be nurtured and protected in a way we just can't imagine right now, because we felt so alone for so long. We've labored under *the illusion* for so long, that (nothing) could happen unless we exerted the 'individual effort.' And what this does is breaks us beyond the illusion of what we are as individuals. And all He's asking us to do, is to focus on the heart — the protective energy that comes from Divine Love. And this Mantle of Protection comes in (actually) knowing that there is a Creator who has loved you ever since you left. And He can't wait for you to come home. And that Love, that recognition of the Divine Love, it's almost like a honing beacon. It's like the magnet that returns you to Him!

"The Love you feel for God is like the thing that brings you home. Because *like attracts like*. You've now magnetized yourself with something, and the thing that it now attracts is Source. I know I'm probably not describing it very well. But the Love of God (and) your feelings of love will pull you through the Passage and (will) act as a homing beacon to bring you Home. 'Cause I was wondering myself that when I was told that love had a protective quality, I wondered how this was possible. But now, the way He's explaining it — that's the analogy right there. It has this magnetic quality to it. Love seeks Love, its own energy. And so when you're enveloping yourself with these feelings of love, feeling love, acknowledging it and filling your heart, then that brings you closer. It's the homing device that brings you back to Source."

Jack then proceeded to ask a question that led to a longer discussion of Singularity:

[Jack: "What's the importance of being able to be in the Love when we leave this physical body? And if we are not feeling the Love when we leave this body, what happens?] "(To extend the movie metaphor), you refuse to go home to your wife and kids. You (just) have to remain on the movie set, even though the film is in the can. You resist being innocent and just acknowledging — letting go of the ego, letting go of all these false facades you've been carrying around for the longest time, and realize that when you break it all down . . . you realize the Wholeness from whence you came. It's like a child. Even though a child (has a knowledge of its exterior physical world), every single child on this earth, subconsciously, knows how much warmer, and homier, and more protected it felt in the womb. Even though it's not consciously known. On a subconscious level, every child knows what it felt like to be in the womb. And similarly, WE all know somewhere deep within our Souls, we know that we all had this Wholeness and this Fullness. But again — AGAIN — we have it in our power to completely ignore that, if we choose. If that wasn't true, we couldn't say that God ever gave us free will. We can understand this on the microcosm of our personal relationships.

"What feels better . . . the girl who really loves you and adores you and wants to be with you because she values you as a person? Or someone you force or pay off to manufacture (loving feelings of) how they feel about you? Do you see the difference? God couldn't have the sense of returning to Himself, if He forced us to Love Him." *[Jack: "It has to be by free will."]* "It had to be by free will. We had to use our volition to complete the circle and come home. So that's why on the relativistic level we might say, 'Well if God is All-Merciful, He could never do that.' However, it's never what God does to us; it's what we do to ourselves. You have it in your power to unite yourself with the dark side, and unite yourself with unreality. But if you do, if you make that decision — collectively — if the soul does that, then it's not part of the Whole. It feels disastrous. Also, the dark side will attempt to portray this in some manner of . . . you know (using an expression that's well-known to 'Trekkies') *'Resistance is futile! You will be assimilated!'* So, you must be part of the contrarian movement. The dark side is going to take advantage of the fact through co-optation that it, itself, initiated. (Consider the following). There are so many people who are turned off by the word 'God.' There are so many people who are turned off by the word 'spiritual.' There are so many people who are turned off by anything having to do with religion, because it's been so abused throughout eons. Therefore, our job is to portray that *our message* transcends all of that. Ours message is not a pro-religious statement. Quite the contrary, it's about what? No more middlemen. Not more intermediaries. It's about the Return. 'And I will speak directly into the Heart of each and every soul.'"

"God wants people to feel the profundity of this message. He challenges us, 'I dare you to come up with anything that is more Fulfilling, that is more Complete, because anything that you can construct artificially will only be some lesser subset of the Whole.' And within Wholeness, remember, there are no subsets (nor is it a subset of anything else) . . . "

[Jack: "You know, for many years, I've realized that the word communication means 'to establish the common unit', and that is Love. I've tried to share, and many people were not capable of feeling that. But now people are able to feel more."] "One of the most important things we're telling people, 'If you will only feel the Love.' There is a *knowingness* in that Love. And out of that knowingness comes the answer to all your questions. *Stop thinking* so much and *start feeling*. You can FEEL Wholeness. You can never intellectually grasp Wholeness, not with the clarity that you can feel it. It's the difference between being in Love and trying to intellectualize it."

Cathryn then asked, "How does this return to Singularity or how does this life on the New Earth affect our concept of money?" Here was the reply:

"Our current concept of money is totally tied to the dark force's co-optation. So, therefore, whatever medium of exchange we use *must* be tied to sharing in this Love and Bliss. It is difficult to portray what that would look and feel like. The exchange of money for goods and services cannot be equated to the exchange of a medium to another human being that you recognize as a part of your own Self. It doesn't feel at all like what we now understand (the principle of money to be). Because when you have a world where the consciousness of the people is such that they're all in Unity Consciousness, the giver and the receiver is *never felt* to be outside of the context of Love. And we can't imagine now what that would look and feel like, because we're just not there yet. We're still in the muck. But, what He's telling me is, every person who reads this will say, 'My God, that feels so right.' For what reason should it be any other way?"

[Jack: "Why would you need money at that point?"] "I'm getting a sense on the New World that there is still exchange. I'll tell you something else about the New Earth. There are still gifts, there are little ingenious ways we figure out to make each other happy and show each other we're special. There are still these things we do to show our emotion, but there is a sense of Fullness of it that we just cannot (now know). When you're in Unity Consciousness, it's a whole other way of Being. Imagine a Society where every single person has full awareness in every moment that they're dealing with aspects of their own Self. We can't even imagine, because to be There, we'd have to all be in Unity Consciousness, and, of course, we're not."

Before closing the session, I had to add one other comment to Cathryn. It concerned a question I had because in all the various spiritual disciplines we had investigated concerning advanced states of consciousness, the goal was always *lofty and distant*. Could the Divine Grace that would unfold throughout 2012 change this? This is what I received:

"In our whole life, on our level of consciousness, enlightenment has been posited as something that is difficult. It can take you lifetimes. Even Buddha used to tell his disciples, I'm going to help you save some time, but it can take you 10,000 more lifetimes. Literally, he would frequently make reference to how arduous the path was. What I'm being shown now is that with His Grace, something that would have taken God-only-knows how many lifetimes, He's going to give us the Help, so that either prior to the Passage or during the Passage — a lot of it's prior — we will be enlightened. We will be in full Unity Consciousness. [Cathryn: "Either prior to or during the Passage?"] Yes, and what's being communicated to me is, He will supply the Grace such that what might have otherwise taken countless lifetimes, will be done in a matter of days, weeks or months.

"And from where I'm at, in this moment, I can tell you that the dark forces — because it couldn't be held back that enlightenment was an actual state of awareness — have attempted to create religions that paint this as an insurmountable and super difficult task. And what's being communicated to me now is, 'There's nothing simpler than being enlightened. You've just made it all complicated.'"

"Among the men and women the multitude,
I perceive one picking me out by secret and
   divine signs,
Acknowledging none else, not parent, wife,
   husband, brother, child, any nearer than I am,
Some are baffled, but that one is not — that one
   knows me.

Ah lover and perfect equal,
I meant that you should discover me so by faint
   indirections,
And I when I meet you mean to discover you by
   the like in you."

~ Walt Whitman — "Among the Multitude"

Chapter 7:

My Love Affair with Ayahuasca

Most of my ayahuasca journeys open up with a set of images that set the *theme* for information that will follow, or there are symbolic representations at the beginning that comprise the "DNA" of the discourse that is to come.

The April 5th session opened up with a myriad of ancient symbols, geometric patterns, and mysterious signs that had been used throughout history — in secret brotherhoods, secret societies, ancient metaphysical schools, and in all manner of occult organizations. The purpose of which was to sequester true knowledge and technology, structure rigid 'common narratives' for population control, gain access to aid from the spirit world, and form alliances with untold realms of inter-dimensional and extra-terrestrial beings. As the images flashed before me, I could tell that there was a movement from the simple to the complex, from ancient to the present day, from symbolism in which a small amount of information was stored, to images in which great knowledge and spiritual significance had been invested. At the same time there was a movement from two dimensional to three dimensional to fourth dimensional to fifth dimensional, and then it exceeded the limits of my neurophysiology: **"Stop! This is more than I can handle!"**

Suddenly, it ended and my consciousness entered a space where I felt I was alone with the ayahuasca plant spirit, which was something I hadn't felt in years. Since 2007 my experiences with ayahuasca felt more "intermediary." It was as if I would encounter *ayahuasca* upon beginning my journey and then she would act as my "switchboard operator," connecting me to other realms. Increasingly, I knew she was always there, somewhere in the background, but we were never alone.

But this was different. Now we felt closer.

Moreover, the feeling and the tone of her presence felt quite different. Strangely, it was a feeling of intense intimacy mixed with a gravitas that gave the sensation that she and I were frozen together in time. The embrace was physical (in sensation), emotional, psychological, and, of course, spiritual. I felt her inside of me and outside of me — a blending of our consciousness as one cannot possibly share with another physical entity or if it's possible, I've never experienced it before.

I realized that Cathryn and Jack were present with me, and they would want to know what I was experiencing. And so I continued . . .

> "**Ayahuasca has seen it all. She has been with us since before Humanity. She herself is an eyewitness to all we have been as a species. And she felt that it was important to communicate that. It's like, 'I have known you from the beginning.' And apparently her reach is quite amazing. When she says she knows us from the beginning, she means every culture, in every land, on every continent, in every time, going back to the very beginning. Her archive alone is it's own Akashic Records[1]. So she herself is this huge repository of knowledge and experience. (She's telling me) 'Just because I'm treating you as a friend, keep in mind what I am.' I guess that's how you'd say it. (Thank you.) She felt it was important to have a more intimate connection with me. (Now she's telling me) 'I have my own perspective about 2012. I could have told you (much of what you've heard). You've gone through all this trouble.'**"

As the session continued, I felt a '*hush*' that penetrated every cell of my body:

> "'**This is a very special moment, because what you don't realize is that this is the end of the mission. This is the end of a mission that's taken me millions of years. You have been on this mission for a matter of a few years, but I have been on my mission, my assignment, for millions of years.'** *[Speaking to Cathryn and Jack]* **I don't know if this is impacting you even a fraction of what it is me. I have no idea what the two you are experiencing in this moment.** *[Cathryn: "It's incredible."]* **She herself is anticipating this, (the Passage). She sees this as hugely momentous because even she as a plant spirit, doesn't know *exactly* (what to think of this, but she knows it to be momentous), because her range of experience is far greater than that of us, as humans. I can't even begin to tell you the range of her experience. She is magnificent. She controls her own universe. In fact, what she controls *is* a universe. She is**

---

1   See glossary.

in a sense, a god. You should respect that. (But) even she is in awe of what is about to happen.

"What she and I are doing now, spiritually, is like two old friends toasting, having a vodka together — however you wish to (see it). It's something on that order of things. She's wanting to connect with me. She is saying, 'Do you understand how important this moment is? Do you understand the moments that we have together — now going forward, how precious and rare they are? Can you even begin to sense (its importance).' Just imagine that for a minute. It's mind boggling. So this is — hold on (I'm seeing) the vast fields of souls she has known. You wouldn't believe it; (it's) millions of people. And the seekers who have come through her portal! So all these incredible experiences that she has a memory of, she doesn't have anyone to share it with — and then I come along. Can you imagine how she responds to me? 'I don't want to pass you off (yet), I want to spend a moment with you first. Can you respect (that)?' She's trying to relate this so you know why she's not so anxious to send me off to Source, because she knows how to get there. I don't need anyone else but her (to transport my consciousness to other realms). She knows the hot line to get directly where we want to go. Now she's saying, 'Please take just a moment to appreciate how unbelievably rare and precious this is. This is the end of the journey for both of us. We should honor this moment.' Are the two of you understanding that?" *[Cathryn and Jack: "Yes." Jack: "I'm getting goose bumps."]*

What follows next is a discussion about what the plant spirits know about 2012, which I cover in another chapter, after which ayahuasca returns to her original theme:

"'The vast, vast spaces in the heavens! The Plants! Many of whom you killed off! You have to understand what happens to a plant after it goes extinct! The spirit of the plant doesn't go away.' In a sense, she mourns the loss of her representation in the third (dimension). Can you feel that? And so, tonight, before we go on, there are things too precious and rare and important for ayahuasca not to take time to relate this. In a sense, she doesn't have anybody else to talk to about this. She feels that this is so important that it should be known by all, and instead of being known by all, it is known by next to nobody. For her to have this — oh my God — (it's a) huge, expansive experience of the entire history of (Earth). Well, she doesn't go back to the start of this planet, but she goes back a very long way. Can you understand the importance of what happens later this year? (What it) would mean to her? And now she's just conveying, you cannot begin to imagine, but 'I felt I had to share it . . . because I don't have anybody else to share it with.' It's pretty unbelievable when you think about it. It's pretty unbelievable what's happening in this room right now, if you can sense what's happening. It's really an honor!

As the session proceeded, the communication from ayahuasca became more emotionally impassioned:

"She told me, 'I have thousands of other visitors . . . coming through my portal. It's not like I don't communicate with many other users. I know the mind and read the mind of each and every person that takes ayahuasca . . . and enters into my domain. I know them all.' What she's telling me is . . . (*oh man, if I can believe this because at this point I feel overwhelmed emotionally*). She says . . . there is something special in the emotional sharing (between us).There are other people who know what's going on, that seek her guidance, and she takes other people to Source all the time. She's saying that my relationship with her is special because . . . hold on . . . this is hard to believe (*there's a long pause*) she's actually honored to be central to these communications . . . (because) there are other plant spirits that are entheogens, right? Magic mushrooms, psilocybin, peyote . . . they all have their own spirits. But she's saying that it's actually an honor that she was able to be the link in all this. 'Just as you were chosen, I was chosen. You could have used other portals. You could have used other entheogens. But I feel grateful that I was chosen.' . . . (*pause as I'm near the point of weeping*). You just have no idea how powerful she is. How BEAUTIFUL she is! She doesn't have a physical form. I've never seen a woman or anything. But she controls her own universe. And what an unbelievably beautiful universe it is! If you could see her domain . . . The vast majority of other users do not see her interior (with the detail and richness) that I see it. So apparently I am, as it were, being given a glimpse of her interior domain. It's unbelievable. She is saying (again), 'Hold this moment precious — you and your friends because — we have business to do, (things) to take care of. Hold this moment, in the time/space continuum, hold it precious, *because there will NEVER be another one like it.'* Can you feel any of this, Jack? Again, it's degrees of intensity?" *[Jack: "We are grateful for her sharing so deeply."]*

[Jack: "I would remind you that there's so little time, and we are grateful to her for sharing."] **"Yes, it's like, 'I'm sharing this with you now because — for whatever reason . . . because I will not be able to share this with you in the future.' This is a flavor of earn this, value this, be grateful and understand its rarity . . ."**

As I continued, I felt her leave my presence, and there were moments of such intense feelings where my communications are, at times, disjointed:

"**Value this, and in a sense I guess this is why she did what she did tonight. I think that in a way she felt that I was taking her for granted. By the way, she's not present at the moment. She's left me in this void. She's making whatever connection . . . I can feel her absence. Before, I was right there with her. She was embracing me. I could feel her. Now she's off, doing things, in preparation for whatever happens later tonight. And I'm in a void right now. She's left me alone in — I won't say a *room* because it's limitless and infinite. I'm in an infinite room. I know that makes no sense. (But) I'm in a room that has infinite space and no walls.** *[Jack: "Greg, can we try something?"]* **Okay, but just realize right now I'm not travelling. I'm in a room. I'm in my altered state, of course; I'm in a sense of anticipation. I'm waiting for her to come back."**

The 'thread' of thought is broken by an interjected question which Jack poses, and then a boundless energy emerges into my consciousness.

"**Hold on . . . Source has been there all the time. In a sense, Source has a Love for his Creation that you cannot even imagine. So even Source was willing to take a backseat . . . It's like your child really wants cotton candy, and you know it's not good for them. You know it's not good for their teeth. But your son or daughter is so enthralled with (the) opportunity to get cotton candy so you, as a parent, say, 'Okay.' So to** this point Source has communicated, 'This is important. This is a big party, so how could I possibly deny ayahuasca the chance to (share in this)'. . . He just has compassion for all His Creation. He has enormous compassion for the plant spirits, too, and so He/She is saying, 'Everything has its time. You don't know how everything is scripted.' My heart is expanding (so much) in this moment! 'I am the architect of all of This and you just don't know it!' He has used people because they were part of the Grand Plan. That's why the Elite of this world are just . . . You have no idea how badly whipped they are. They don't understand. Again, this is continuation of what we talked about two nights ago. They can't pull themselves out of the character (mode). They don't recognize that.

"Source is the architect of everything . . . As much as we would describe our sense of human affection, His affection for ayahuasca. (Wow!) I am getting the sense of His immense affection for ayahuasca, because He created her. And there's this kind of special bond between them because she's been the guardian of this portal through which otherwise a lot of humans, myself included, might not have known Him or communicated with Him. So, in a sense, Source has a special relationship with her because she has been His *(pause)* translator? Facilitator? Perhaps facilitator is a better word. (His) facilitator through eons. So even now, it's mutual. Both she and Source want me to understand and respect their special relationship . . . The time line is short. We don't have much time, Jack. But we have enough time to share this moment. Is any of this making sense? *[Cathryn and Jack: "Yes."]*

There are no words to describe my awareness of the presence of Source with ayahuasca. Imagine a father looking down with the most loving eyes on a most beloved daughter. He is looking down at her with nothing but love and affection, and she is looking back at him with nothing but love and pride. The experience was akin to this but amplified many times over.

Shortly after this segment, the entire nature of the session ended, and Source took over. It was "back to business." In the vision quests that followed I never again shared anything again that was similar to that one, special, all-loving, experience with the ayahuasca plant spirit. In reflecting back on the collage of symbols and images that opened the session, I realized that this was but a small sampling of the things to which she had been an eyewitness throughout the ages.

She was right. We would continue our work, but that one moment of reflection, which (for her) incorporated millions of years, the shared experiences with millions of souls over countless eons, would remain a special moment, frozen in time.

For both of us.

"Sure as the ship of all, the Earth itself,
Product of deathly fire and turbulent chaos,
Forth from its spasms of fury and its poisons,
Issuing at last in perfect power and beauty . . . "

~ Walt Whitman — "O Star of France"

Chapter 8:

The New & Old Earths

The last two sessions in April took place on the 23rd and 28th — where much of the vision questing focused on differences between the Old (or 'devolved') and the New Earth, as well as the relationship between the Passage and the "Split" itself.

The most significant revelation of April 28th had to do with the unique nature of the "Passage" as a preparation for the Split. This hit me hard and struck me as another facet of the "unfoldment" — namely, that information was being withheld until key junctures along the time line leading up to the Passage. Prior to this vision quest I had specifically asked for details about the relationship between the Passage and the Split, and I had received very little information. It wasn't even clear to me what their causal relationship were.

After forty minutes into my April 28th journey, that changed.

"If you took all the experiences that you had, from the time you first decided to meditate and turn to God, to the time you actually became enlightened — *these three days are a truncation of that.*

"I'm being shown this tunnel. Remember we talked about the horse speeding up? You're going to feel like you're going down a tunnel, and you're actually going to be able to experience a preview of what that feels like (during the Passage). And it's like everything I've already told you; the analogy of the horse speeding up — focusing on love as you're going through it — returning to Source, because that's what brings you home. All that (prior communication)? But IN ADDITION to that, these three days are a truncation (of the evolutionary process). This is where God's Divine Grace comes in, because this is a gift. In those three days, you're going through all of the processes you would have gone through (even) if God wasn't saying 'enough is enough.' And He was going to let you continue on

(incarnating) for the next 50 or 100 lifetimes — or whatever (time span it would take) 'til you finally get enlightened. This three day period is a truncation of that in order to get the job done. This is a speeding up of the process, that you would ordinarily take many more lifetimes to (attain) complete Unity Consciousness. And He's showing me is that there are many different flavors of enlightenment. I've known about that. Maharishi talked about that, but now I'm actually experiencing it. It's not like, there's unenlightened and enlightened. Far from it, there's actually layers of complete enlightenment. To the 'nth degree' (this) full Unity Consciousness, this three days should be appreciated. That's what makes it such a gift; (it) is because it's a truncation of that process. And so that's why there's all these intense feelings about things being sped up, because — as it pertains to spiritual evolution — this is an enormous speeding up of the normal process . . ."

This revelation struck me as so important that I couldn't stop myself from addressing this point as a side comment.

"**And I don't know why we weren't told that sooner.** [Cathryn: *"We were told we were going to receive revelations sequentially as part of the unfoldment."*] **Yes, but to me that's such an essential point.** [Cathryn: *"We've unfolded to the point where we can receive that particular information."*] **That's what makes this period such a gift. That's what makes it so rare. And that's what would make it unfortunate, if we can't get people to** *wake up* **to it. This is such an enormous gift . . . 'Don't you want to undo the ribbon, look in the box, and see what it is?'** [Cathryn: *"Yes."*] **. . . (or) 'The end of 2012 is the biggest gift you'll ever receive in your life. Because it's coming around Christmas time, wouldn't it be a shame if you didn't undo the ribbon, open the box, and see what it is? Don't you want to know what it is?'"**

"**What I'm really feeling and experiencing in this session is what a truly, rare gift this thing is that's coming upon us.** *The Passage.* **What I call the Passage. What an enormous gift it is, because you're going to be able to use those three days to bypass unbelievable future lifetimes that were scheduled for you. Now you don't have to go through (them).**

[Cathryn: *"That's amazing."*] **"He's giving me another**

analogy. If you're in a very special school and you have a very gifted teacher, you have the ability to say either, 'I'm here. I know what an incredible gift this is. I'm going to listen to everything my teacher tells me. I know that He's a remarkable instructor, and I have so much to learn.' Or you (could) sit in the classroom and say, 'Look. I just want to get through this. I'm going to fake it. I'm going to pretend that I'm listening. I'm going to do whatever I have to do because I'm just trying to get through it.' And, again, what He's saying is, 'Surely you must know that the experience of those two students is entirely different.' So this gets back to the Aesop fable. The experience of winter is totally different for the grasshopper than it is for the ant. The importance of this session tonight — what the Divine is trying to do is to emphasize to a degree we had not previously contemplated — (is communicate) the *importance of preparation*."

When I thought back to the revelation about sequential unfoldment between past life review, past incarnational reviews on this and other parallel universes, and the review of humanity's collective past, I couldn't help but comment:

"There's an aspect of this — I'm almost thinking — even if I wasn't being told this outright, couldn't we have figured this out on our own?" *[Cathryn: "Uh-uh." and Jack: "No, not if it's a gift."]*

During this same session, I received another analogy as to why I wouldn't have received this message sooner in my vision quests. I call this one the "focusing telescope metaphor" (or *telescope metaphor*), which ends in yet another reference to "the Christmas metaphor":

"You have to believe there is this unfolding such that every time we have a session, there is something more profound coming out ... and it's like looking at something through a telescope and trying to focus, so you can see it crystal clear. Well, if you were to chop up the process into 50 different stages, at each stage, it gets a little bit clearer. As you keep turning the knob, the image gets clearer and clearer, until you get to a point where, 'That's it. No More. This is perfect.' Any more tampering with the focusing knob is now unproductive, because you can't get any better than crystal clear. Ok, so what I'm being told is, the sessions (we) going through are like that. We are tuning, tuning, tuning, (as) part of the unfoldment . . . until we'll get to a point where everything is crystal clear. But even then it won't be the same as *feeling* crystal clarity, (That) won't come until Christmas."

Seeing the Passage not merely as an alteration in time-space, but as an enormous act of Divine Grace, led to the following — the beginning of which was a commentary on my part more than anything channeled:

"What we're telling people is, 'There's going to be an opportunity to experience the (Wholeness) as you go through this, but you have to prepare yourself. Imagine if you started seeing these (past life) flashes and you didn't know that it was your time to have a past life review. You'd be completely lost. You might go crazy . . . It's going to become more apparent as we proceed through this year. Preparing people and saying, 'Listen, (Source is) going to give you the opportunity in the span of three little days to fast-forward through an unbelievable number of lifetimes so that you can come Home.' And you know what? Tonight is the first night where I realized that the three days served that function. That essentially what's happening. If things were left to their own devices, there's no telling how many more lifetimes we'd go through in order to get to Unity. These three days are — among everything else we're experiencing — the opportunity to speed us up."

"It's this crash course preparation. And if you can get through it and get your lessons, you can stay on track. For the first time I'm being shown this — this split between the *New and old* Earth is at the conclusion of (the Passage). It can't happen prior.

"At the conclusion of the Passage, there will be those who experience it in accordance with the way that God designed it. For those who take advantage of the opportunity, there is this personal metamorphosis. You are transformed, and that's why — and I've been sensing this all along — we are not the same people we are now. You can't combine yourself with all the other fragments of who you are and stay the person you are right now.

"So — it *is* about personal transformation. It's an ENORMOUS growth opportunity. And those butterflies who get out of the cocoon, who go to the New World, who can follow this and follow what its purpose is, (and) who are transformed will go to an Earth that is itself transformed. And those who don't, or who ignore it, it's a real mess for them. It's this *old earth*. It's this — oh man — hold on, I'm being shown something and I have to get a sense of what this is . . ."

"As I've said before, the vast majority of my sessions involve clairaudience, not clairvoyance. It is for this reason that when I am shown something visual, I will normally stop anything else I'm focusing on and devote myself to the new visual. What was shown to me was the *devolved* Earth well after the Split and what was transpiring:

"For the first time I'm being shown this old Earth . . . it's this coalescing of soul fragments. Oh my God, even on the other parallel worlds, this old Earth, the grey one? . . . I wasn't sure if the Singularity drew all the (soul fragments) . . . it's hard to describe what I'm being shown . . . in the negative way, that's what makes it so evil and lifeless, because basically this Old Earth is like the ultimate cosmic trash can. And what I'm being told, when you cultivate all this evil, with all these Elitists and all their millions of minions, who will gladly sell their soul to the devil for their 30 pieces of silver? (Well) that has its own magnetic force. Evil attracts evil. 'I have used My devoted Angelic Messengers, including the Archangels, to protect (you from your) own folly,' so that souls who are like those of us in this room could make it to the end zone. After this happens, there's this Split — there's a separation — (and) that magnetic effect (will be enhanced), because 'I will remove all support.' This Old Earth (devolved earth) becomes a hell beyond your wildest imagination. Because, unbeknownst to us, there has been this *Divine Influence*, without which, *this world would be far worse* than it is now. That's hard for you and I to believe, but it would be even worse."

"(Source wants us too understand), 'If you want to experience pure evil, pure selfishness, pure greed, let's see what this feels like when I have withdrawn ALL angelic support, all support from the Divine . . . And let it be the magnet that it is, and let it draw from throughout the multiverse even unto the other parallel universes . . .' Again, it's hard to describe, what I'm seeing in terms of what this event is . . . *(long pause)* . . . I had no idea when we started this project that it was so momentous. I thought it was special but I didn't think it was (this momentous)." *[Jack: "So instead of celebrating a Happy New Year, we're going to celebrate a Happy New World."]*

When I first began receiving messages in March that I should take the communications I'd received, organize them, and produce a book, I thought I had a clear understanding of what I was doing. Even by that time I had received enough information to know that relative to other revelations about 2012, this was a clearer, more distinct, unified vision of "2012's end." However, with the information I had just received, even my own perception of what I was doing had been turned on its head. I interjected the following into the session to record what I was experiencing:

"This book is a guidebook to getting you through the Passage successfully. And I'm getting the sense we're going to be getting more information over the next couple of sessions. You cannot put into human words the difference between getting through it successfully, and not making it. There's no words we're going to be able to come up with that can convey, 'What is the difference between the soul that makes it and the soul that doesn't?' We can describe it on several levels. The most basic, is the very point we make in Chapter One. This is an astrophysical event. You can understand the human body experiencing different things because it will be subjected to these high intensity frequencies that it has never been subjected to before. Now you (can) take it to the next level of understanding. Realize that those who understand this (in spiritual terms have a more comprehensive grasp of the Event). Again, we're staying on a very basic astrophysical paradigm to explain it as opposed to using more spiritual terms. Can you understand the difference for a person who is prepared to receive those frequencies, knows it's coming, knows play-by-play what will happen next and knows what to expect? They have been working to prepare for it. Can you imagine how much different that person's experience will be from somebody who doesn't have knowledge about it at all? Or who has only a very superficial knowledge of it? It's a very powerful thing that's being communicated."

"I'm getting a greater appreciation of what this book is about than I had before tonight. *[Cathryn: "Well, it's coming together"]* This is a PLAYBOOK! Imagine you went to a football game. You don't really know much about the game. You know that there's two teams, but you don't even understand that when you get to the end zone that you get points; that's the (object) of the game. You don't even understand its purpose! You just went to a football game because a friend asked you to go. But somehow, someway you got through your childhood and you actually didn't know what the rules of the game are. Can you imagine the difference between that and someone who goes, who's a fan, knows the names of the players, all the rules and technicalities and everything else? Can you imagine the huge, vast differences between their experiences?"

Later in the session, the concept was expanded upon, including the addition of an analogy equating the Passage to getting through high school.

"This enormous gift that we're going to be given — to get people to have this miniaturization in terms of the time continuum — this is probably a poor analogy of the feelings I'm being given. It would be like you're a senior in high school and you have to pass this series of exams. If you don't pass the exams, which are not very difficult, you don't get to graduate. They set the threshold pretty low, because they want to get the majority of students through. Despite that, if you don't pass the exams, you don't get your diploma. In a sense, we're all in that situation or we wouldn't be re-incarnating back on this particular planet and so forth."

"It's as if what God is doing, is saying, 'I'm going to create a crash course to get you people ready, if you're willing to come Home, if you are one with the Divine Heart and you realize that it's time to come Home,' that this crash course serves as preparation. I did not understand before tonight this causal relationship between the three days of darkness and the earth splitting. Was there any connection at all? And what I'm seeing tonight is this a *profound interconnection*. The results of the Passage sets up the conditions for the Split."

"Moreover, (the Passage occurs) on so many levels of Creation; some of which are just too difficult for me to try to describe, because I can't describe something that even I don't fully understand. The gross physical phenomenon itself, the Passage, is nothing compared (to the unseen aspects of this phenomena). If you could see what I see because Creation is this incredible multi-layered cake — if you could see the subtlety of it throughout Creation — it's like this collapse. It looks and feels like everything is all over the place and now everything has to be herded. It's like a discotheque, packed with a thousand people and you've got one tiny fire escape, and someone yells, 'Fire.' Can you imagine everyone in this huge establishment trying to get through one small door, (and) going down the fire escape to get out because of the fire? That's what it looks and feels like. It's like this herding into the Singularity. I don't know any other way to describe it."

The following passage was received about a specific question that Jack asked in reference to the galactic center.

"Creation went out (as I've said to you in previous readings) and became fragmented, fragmented, fragmented. (Now), it's ready to return to where it started in the first place.' It went so far out and then God said, 'Alright. I wanted to see where this would go.' This is all happening within the Mind of God. Now He's seen it, and now He's had enough. Now let's bring it back to where it started from.' Do you get that sense? And so, to get back to your original question, Jack, it's like, 'Yes, you could ascribe to it a (kind of) photon belt.' But really on deeper levels there's so much more to it than that. It's almost like something for us to focus on because if we can't understand something going on in the 3rd dimensional realm, then it's too abstract for our tiny monkey brains. So, 'Yes, it's a photon magnet,' but that's only one thin layer in a huge multi-layer cake in His Creation."

"On so many levels, it's so much bigger than that, and at subtle levels closer to the Divine, it's far more purposeful. Because, even as we go through this, your scientific minds are going to be going, 'It's okay. We'll pass through it. 2013's going to be a great year.' Okay, they're not going to get it. They're going to stay on that level, that relativistic mind, but for them it's only a gross physical event. And in a way, I'm getting this sense that God has this almost as a way to bait us to try to get us interested, to try to get our attention as to the importance of what needs to happen. But to Him, and

I think I said this in one of the last two sessions, it's like, 'Forget all that. I would do this even if there wasn't a Photon Belt. I've had enough.' Yes, this is as we've described in the very beginning of Chapter One, about the Passage. But on subtler levels of Creation, it is so much more. And its purpose is so much richer and deeply pregnant with significance than just some gross (phenomenon) which is (similar) to a solar eclipse, but just a little bit more important. To imagine that we are to embark upon (something which) is the conclusion of an entire act of Creation. You just can't begin to imagine."

"(We need to understand) the deep significance of these three days of darkness in terms of our participation in it and our need to be prepared. Because if we're not prepared, a person's going to enter this and he's going to be completely unable to accept the opportunity of what (he) can experience going through it."

[Cathryn: "The New Earth. Where does it end up? Are there going to be dimensions or is it going to be Singularity/ Source?"] **"No. It's a Singularity. There's no question about it in my mind, based on what I'm being shown.** *[Cathryn: "So it's not like a 5th dimension or a higher dimension?"]* **All this talk about (moving into the) 5th dimension, that's just a focus on a tiny fragment. No, this is a grand cosmic contraction. It's going to feel like a contraction."**

As the session progressed, I got the distinct sense the Divine felt that the experience of the Passage hadn't been sufficiently communicated so that a reader could get a "feel" or a "sense" for him/herself. Sure enough, along came another cosmic metaphor, but this was — as least as I felt it upon receiving it — more concrete than anything else that had been communicated to me. I found it so compelling that I now refer to it as the "Hourglass Analogy."

"Let me tell you something else, in terms of the laws of physics. Imagine looking at a large hourglass, the kind used to measure time before there were clocks. Think of the experience in the upper globe as seen from the consciousness of one grain of sand, sitting near the top, next to the glass. At first it doesn't appear that much of anything is going on, right? You just don't feel anything. You may not even accept that you're moving. 'I'm sitting here. I'm not going anywhere. I'm happy right where I am.' Then the next realization is, 'Wait a minute, guys. We're moving down. Relative to the glass we're moving down.' And then the next realization is that the center is more significant than the periphery. Now compare all of that to the experience of passing from the upper globe to the lower the globe. The speed! Can you imagine that difference from the perspective of the consciousness of that single grain of sand?

"That's where we are. We're in the hourglass of time. And when the book comes out, we're going to be telling people, the center of the hourglass is more significant than out here on the periphery. This is significant.'

"But even that, as much as we (tell) people to help prepare them for what's to come, is not as significant as the experience that the sand has at the point where it passes that tiny juncture between the upper and the lower globes — when it no longer represents time. It goes from "potential time" to "time past." And the experience that the sand has going through that tiny juncture — and then the *speed* of it! Up here he (the grain) wasn't even willing to acknowledge he was moving. Then compare that to the speed of the Passage, for we've all seen what happens to sand as it's passing through an hourglass. That's what this will be like compared to now, where we're not even moving (to) the incredible speed as we're going through the Passage."

"To get the comparison you almost have to enter into the consciousness of that tiny grain of sand. All grains of sand have their own consciousness. That's a whole other (discussion) . . . That's how important this is. That's the *experience* you have going through it. It would be a whole lot easier, if the grain of sand knew from the very beginning, 'Look. I'm already ready for this. I know the importance of the center. I know where this goes. I even know that there's a globe on the bottom where we're still going to be grains of sand. Instead of being on the top globe, we're going to be on the bottom globe.' Imagine how much difference the experience would be, even unto the consciousness of a grain of sand, if he knew all of that before he went through it, instead of being surprised and bewildered about the whole thing.

"This is radical. This is like you just got on the roller coaster and it's going to go from 0 to 600 mph in milliseconds. *[Cathryn: "Wow."]* You're on a roller coaster. Get prepared for a whole different world of experience. Time, as we know it, doesn't exist. It's like the movie, *The Matrix*, where in 30 seconds (of information transferral) you are able to do something that it would take you days, if not weeks, of training. But you've just downloaded it in a matter of a few seconds. That's what this is like. *[Cathryn: "Instead of taking months to master how to fly a helicopter, it's done in seconds."]* **Correct.**"

MOTHER EARTH MOVES TO THE NEW EARTH

Until April 28th, I had never encountered the spirit of Mother Earth. I had seen glimpses of this magnificent entity, especially when walking quietly through the cloud forests of the high Andes, where I live. However, never before had I experienced a clear, personal encounter, the way I had so often with the ayahuasca plant spirit. My encounter with 'Pachamama'[(1)] led to an entirely new realization about the nature of the Split. Just as my understanding of the causal relationship between the Passage and the Split — and even the purpose of this very book — was altered by this session, so, too, was my understanding of the nature between Mother Earth as a spiritual entity and the New Earth.

On the cover of this book you will see a graphic that shows the earth splitting into two — an Old Earth on the left and a vibrant New Earth on the right. I had an artist compose this graphic because this is precisely as I had seen it in January. It looked to me like a cell going through mitosis. The information I received from Mother Earth didn't change this perception, but it greatly expanded it.

"The Old Earth? The devolved earth? Are you ready for this? *It's this one* — (the one we are on now). The New Earth comes out of this. Mother Earth gives birth, and out of her pain, with the help of the Creator, (she gives birth from) the earth that we're on right now? This earth? We're living on the devolved earth right now. It just hasn't gotten really bad yet — as bad as it's going to get.

"I'm being shown that. So it splits. It's this splitting. But the devolved earth part of the split and the templates for it are already here now, alive and well, and demonically running the

_____
1   Pachamama is a goddess revered by the indigenous people of the Andes. Pachamama is usually translated as (spirit of) Mother Earth, but a more literal translation would be "Mother World."

show. **Okay?** *[Cathryn: "Uh-huh"]* **This is a very, very distinct experience that I'm going through. The —** *oh my God!* **— I'm experiencing Mother Earth as an actual spirit. We always talk about Mother Earth being an organism. I'm experiencing Mother Earth as a spirit, and let me tell you something, there are a lot of things coming out tonight that are really profound. But what she's showing me is that when this Split happens, with this great Mercy of God, she's coming with us on the New Earth. So this devolved earth is soulless. Does that make any sense? It's spiritless.** *[Jack: "Like leaving the shell behind. Like when a locust sheds its skin or a snake."]*

"And the New Earth, she lives with us, and the old earth is soulless . . . I'm being shown that Mother Earth — keep in mind that we're talking about the heart chakra of the universe — as a spirit, is in such pain that I can actually feeling her weeping. Mother Earth does have a distinctly feminine feel to her, very motherly, very grand, and what I'm able to feel is enormous compassion from the Creator. And I feel as I go deeper into this — maybe this is just another coincidence, I don't know — it's like God can feel her weeping. The Split, among all its other properties and characteristics, is God swooping down, taking the tender hand of Mother Earth, pulling her out of hell, and bringing her to paradise.

"You know the pain that we feel, having to remain on this earth? Well what I'm being shown right is that Mother Earth (as an spirit) is experiencing the same thing. You don't want to be on this earth? Mother Earth doesn't want to be on this earth (either)! Can you appreciate that? *[Cathryn: "Yes."]* So among all these other things going on, Mother Earth's desire to depart is another part of the energetics of the Split. Imagine the spirit of a planet not wanting to reside on that planet, just wanting nothing to do with it. Earth, the physical manifestation of what she is! She wants to get (out, too)! Mother Earth has a spirit, has these personality characteristics that you can see — if you're awake. (They) are all over the planet, in all of her life forms. She is very tender; she's very compassionate; she's playful; she's occasionally impish; she's creative; she can experience pride with something she's created, and she's really an enormous spirit in terms of her capabilities. The whole idea that she wants to leave her own planet, is like us not wanting to be in our bodies and wishing we could die and take another form. Well, imagine on a planetary level, that things have reached a point where the conditions on her planet are so contrary to her Nature that even she doesn't want to be here.

"I was asking about her interior. There are other civilizations below the surface of the earth. And what she's telling me is, 'Most of my interior isn't much better.' Not just on the surface, but on all these other levels. Different civilizations — some on other dimensions — that run (live) in the interior of the earth. And that nowhere in my physical manifestation is there a paradise, despite what you may have read. So, she knows what is about to happen. And I'll tell you something else, she knows (for whatever reason), and has a knowledge and appreciation of what's happening that is even greater than the plant spirits. She's anticipating this. *[Jack: "Doesn't she have vortices and special places upon the earth where the energy flows better?"]* Well, none of that really matters, because when the earth is this negative, even these special places, these vortices, they are living at this dramatic minimization of what their real potential is — the full expression of their purpose. So, again, it's this dramatic Split. It's coming to a point where this whole *good versus evil* confrontation that's been going on throughout the entirety of Creation (has to end). Every conflict has a beginning and an end. This conflict started shortly after Creation because God allowed it for his purposes. It has to have an end. The Passage is the beginning of the end."

Later in the session I came to realize that in our current relativistic mind, it is nearly impossible to imagine life on a "soulless planet." I lamented for those who would make bad choices and have to experience it.

"I am confounded by the view of Mother Earth reigning over her manifestation of a new, purified, renewed Earth, casting off one that is then soulless. I don't even know how that's possible, because when I take my consciousness and look at other planets . . . all planets have a spirit. If the spirit wasn't there, the planet wouldn't have manifested. It's like us. We have human bodies, but once we leave, the flesh just decomposes. It's because of (a human) spirit that this body is given life and becomes animated. And because our spirit gives this flesh life and animates it . . . we animate flesh that otherwise (would be lifeless) . . . So (I have to ask myself) what's going to animate the old earth? That's why I don't think people know what they're getting themselves into. Imagine living on a soulless planet. It's just the carcass. The spirit has left."

Later in the session, I examined what this would mean from another spiritual perspective:

"One needs to pay attention once understanding the deep spiritual significance of the Passage. 'Enter through the narrow gate. For wide is the gate and broad is the road that leads to destruction . . .' because it *is* destruction. To have all of God's power removed — that protects us — and then to be on a planet where the spirit of the planet has left. Whatever hell we're living in now, can you imagine what kind of hell it will be after we go through this?" *[Cathryn: "How can anything live when the goal of the One World Order is just to destroy and murder and control? What's going to be left to control?"]*

When I posed Cathryn's final question to the Divine, I found it puzzling that I got no response. I got nothing. Only silence. It was only after I transcribed the recording the next day that I gathered the wisdom to understand that this *was* the answer to her final question.

Nothing.

GARDENING ON THE NEW PLANET

"Let me tell you what gardening is going to be like on the New Earth. This is profound. Imagine gardening where you can speak to your plants and hear what your plants are 'saying' to you. (Imagine feeling) your plants' knowingness of your presence. That you are their gardener. Imagine what that would feel like? This is what's being shown to me. *[Cathryn: "Be such an honor."]* Imagine gardens more full of life than anything we can imagine now. We are able to nourish our plants with our thoughts because our prayers will be amplified. So our plants actually look forward to our presence, because they know that we have the power with our prayer, our prayerful thought, to enrich them. I can tell you that gardens are much fuller and vibrant — there's no other way to describe it, than they are now.

"Beautiful gardens are another manifestation of God's desire to know Himself. On a deep level, within every soul — somewhere on a deep level we know — that there is something enormously aesthetic and beautiful about being in a magnificent garden. The relationship we have with our plants, wanting to nourish them, to know them, and feel them nourish us back, is a (harmonic) of what's happening between the Creator and human souls."

MORE ON OUR RELATIONSHIP WITH ANIMALS ON THE NEW EARTH

The subject of our relationship with animals in the New Earth had already come up in an earlier session, but after the spontaneous commentary about gardens, the topic surfaced again. This time additional insights were added.

[Cathryn: "What is our relationship with animals in the New World"]. "Well, it's really enhanced. They understand us. We understand them. The relationship we have with animals is far more intimate. It even feels more intimate than the way that Anastasia[2] describes it. Remember the wolf and the bear? How the animals helped her in raising her son? All those things that she talks about are going to be commonplace."

[Cathryn: "How do animals take care of themselves? Because Anastasia said that the animals took care of themselves. People did not have to take care of them."] "Well in an enlightened culture, society has a certain energetics to it, which it radiates into its surroundings, and one of the by-products of the emanation of that enlightened consciousness is that the animals are able to feel their place. I mean, before there were large sections of the earth that were very sparsely populated by humans. How did the (undomesticated) animals tend for themselves then? They obviously did or we wouldn't have any animals. So, their ability to function in terms of Mother Nature's original intent or the Divine's original intent is enhanced in the presence of an enlightened society."

[Cathryn: "Well, do animals still eat other animals, eat plants or are they breatharians[3]?"] "(If) I have to cover every species

2 Ringing Cedars: *Anastasia* Book 1 by Vladimir Megré (http://www.ringingcedars.com/books/)
3 See Breatharianism at Wikipedia (https://en.wikipedia.org/wiki/Inedia)

of animal I can think of ... I'd rather make a broad statement about what I'm feeling than going through each species. Obviously you have animals that are carnivores. You have animals that are herbivores. What I'm seeing is that the whole environment is changed. (Just as) this is a very profound transformation for us, it's a very profound transformation for the animals, as well. Just as we go through these dramatic changes as we are subjected to all these frequencies, going back to our 3rd dimensional paradigm, all these frequencies that human beings are subjected to, animals are likewise subjected to them. They go through profound changes, too. *[Cathryn: "Ok."]* **We just haven't talked about it up to this point, because our focus has been humanity.**

"The animal world is transformed. Just as we have a profound enhancement to our perceptual capabilities, so, too, animals — which would only make sense. Communication between two different species is bilateral. It's not unilateral. It isn't just about our capabilities; it's about theirs, too. If I say something to my dog, and my dog understands me — where he wouldn't have before — it is the animal that has had an increase in their perceptual awareness. But because of their innocence, they do not have to prepare for this. The rules are entirely different for them than (they are) for us. We've been given so much, and so much will be expected of us. We have the opportunity to live in God's Mind. That's unique because the plant and animal spirits won't have that. They understand the significance of what we're about to go through. (However) at the end of this, even the plant spirits — which have *enormous* capabilities and reach, will not be able to experience what we are capable of, which is to live inside God's Mind."

WILL WE STILL NEED FOOD ON THE NEW EARTH?

[Cathryn: "Will we still require food or will we be like 'God-eaters' and just live off the energy of God?"] **As I've said in a previous reading, there is this speeding up in the growth in evolution that will take place. My sense is that initially there will be eating, but then, very quickly, people will realize how to survive inside that Wholeness. Simply (put), they'll be God-eaters, breatharians. Whereas now, very few souls are able to master this spiritual technique, on the New Earth it will be**

commonplace.

"But there will still be those who (eat). They'll be eating on the New Earth. *[Cathryn: "Vegetarian?"]* Yes ... primarily because things will be such that you'll be able to feel this intimacy with animals — remember, you'll be able to talk to animals. So why would you want to kill something that you are able to so intimately communicate with? It's not anything that's enforced. People (will) just have a natural desire to do that." Similarly, the move to breatharianism is a natural result of our increased intimacy with plants, coupled with a collective ability to sustain ourselves without their consumption."

THE NATURE OF DEATH/DIFFERENT PHYSICAL MANIFESTATIONS

[Cathryn: "So, once we make it to the New Planet . . . when people die, is there still going to be reincarnation to the New Earth?"] "People pass on . . . it looks like everybody's got a rainbow body. People when they leave . . . they have a knowledge when it's time to depart and return to experiencing God's Love and Bliss in a bodiless way. There is no sadness attached to it. It doesn't look like there's a body to bury. I don't see any cemeteries. This is so weird. I don't see any cemeteries. And I'm looking."

[Cathryn: "When we go through the Passage, there's only going to be One Universe, no more parallel universes, but there's still going to be multiple planets . . . we were talking about experiencing God's Love on Earth. Are there going to be other places or other planets I should say with God's Love or is it just planet Earth?"] "We will be able to go to other planets and other worlds. I'm being shown a planet that you and I lived on and spent a long time on. It has this purple hue to it. It's bigger than our Earth. (It) seems like our bodies are bigger, too. It's very beautiful . . . similar to Earth. We breathe oxygen. I can see the clouds. That's where we lived. That was our home planet."

[Cathryn: "You were saying that souls come to planet Earth to experience God's Love. That's a little bit confusing to me, because to me you should be able to experience God's Love on other planets also."] "And what I'm saying is that you will go to other planets. There will be other places you can go in

the Singularity. But the purpose of taking a physical form will not be the same as it is now."

[Cathryn: "Okay, what will be the purpose of taking a physical form?"] **As I've said in a previous reading and now it's in the book, to experience God's Love and God's Bliss in a different way."**

[Cathryn: "And what's going to be different about it."] **"Well, Cathryn, I can tell you even as I'm travelling right now, the experience of being just a spirit is very different from the experience of owning a physical body. It's a different experience."**

[Cathryn: "So it's just another way of experiencing God's love."] **"Correct."**

[Cathryn: "But we can take on many forms to experience God's Love, correct?"] **"I don't want to put words in His mouth. There's a range of experiences (that) you can have to experience His Love. It's different forms of God, but the consciousness of God never leaves you."**

LOVE ON THE NEW EARTH:
EVEN IN SINGULARITY THERE IS SUBJECT AND OBJECT

"This is another point that I think is kind of important. This is so complex, I don't know how I'm going to express it, because in the unenlightened state of consciousness, it's such a paradox. Love is a kind of manifestation of Wholeness. But when we think of Divine Love, even that is not at the same level as pure Wholeness, because Wholeness is complete within Itself. Even when you say Divine Love, (our) own human understanding of it involves a subject and an object. Love is the transference of feeling from one source to the object of that love. There's a 'subject-object' character to love.

"And this is what I am being told: that's what this New Earth is about. It's easy to think of Singularity (as a folding back) into this absolute, nameless, formless thing. God is God, and it's the end of Creation and all that. But what I'm being told is that within the Singularity itself this (Event) doesn't come to a proper conclusion unless God still has some kind of medium through which there is this relationship between subject and

object. (In this way) Love can be experienced, and there is this kind of dynamic between Creator and created.

"So this New Earth is very special to God, because it allows Him to experience that Divine Love between Creator and created in a purified way, which is why this Split has to happen. I'm being shown a separation between the wheat and the chaff. That which will contribute to the fulfillment of what is Creation's purpose and all the other trash that has to be separated."

OLD EARTH VS NEW EARTH:
SEPARATING THE WHEAT FROM THE CHAFF

"On some level within the Mind of God — and I hate to say this because it really sounds anthropomorphic — it really feels like He's fed up. Do you understand what I'm saying? *[Cathryn: "Uh-huh."]* So this shift, this break, is required because this New Earth can't happen unless you have a place to put all these other people — those who just can't get with the program. *[Jack: "So it's a natural outcome."]* (Yes), if you take water and mix salt with it and make brine, then freeze it, the salt will rise to the top. That's what this feels like.

"God shows me the weirdest analogies. You know what I'm being shown (now)? This is where the chosen aspect gets into it. He was showing me fruit pickers, (where the instruction to workers is), 'You have to pick the right (sized) avocados. If it's too big or it's too small, throw it out. The avocado has to be the right size. It's gotta be the *right market size*. It has to be what the consumer expects.' So it's like souls are being picked and being given special attention — I guess as a decision of the Divine — of those who are ready. 'You have had enough incarnations to figure this out. Haven't you been through enough pain yet?' He's kind of turning the tables, 'You complain how evil the world is, well if it's so evil, don't you get the point? Haven't you been through enough incarnations of hell to realize that you don't belong there?'

"'You belong up here with Me. You don't belong there. You've had enough different roles. You've played enough different characters on enough different planets; you've had enough experiences over enough lifetimes.' He's saying, 'I know from your soul development (where you are).' So God is consciously giving attention to those souls that He feels are going to make the grade — or to use the analogy I just gave you, the avocado that's fit for market size — that's fit to go to the New Earth. And those that aren't — not as much attention is being given to them.

"He wants everybody to make it but the reality is (restating what Archangel Rafael said in the April 10th session) 'most will not'. But still — we have to make the effort. It's almost as if even unto God, He wouldn't feel right if every effort wasn't made right up to the last second to try to get people to take a genuine interest in 'Why am I here? What is my purpose? And isn't it time to go home?'"

"We consider the bibles and religions divine . . . .
I do not say they are not divine,
I say they have all grown out of you and may
grow out of you still,
It is not they who give the life . . . . it is you who
give the life;
Leaves are not more shed from the trees or
trees from the earth than they are shed out of
you."

~ Walt Whitman — "A Song for Occupations"

Chapter 9:

Co-Creation to the Point of Passage

M uch of the material communicated in the later half of April had to do with issues related to "preparation" as it pertained to the Passage. Some of these communications came spontaneously, and others came as a result of questions asked.

One response that was unexpected concerned the role of nutrition as it relates to preparation. Although important, the Divine emphasized that preparation as it relates to the heart is far *more* important. That mimicked the Christian concept that "what comes of out the mouth is more important than what goes into it":

THE ROLE OF NUTRITION IN PREPARATION FOR THE PASSAGE

> [*"Cathryn: In preparation to go forward through these changes is nutrition important? Should we eat a certain way to prepare the body? Or is it more about the heart?]* **"He's saying it's more about the heart. He's not saying, 'don't eat right.' Try to void artificiality; I guess He means processed foods. Try to eat things that are whole as much as possible. Try to eat things that are whole because this *is* about Wholeness. Foods are better (if eaten) in their pristine state. Instead of buying apple sauce, eat an apple. Instead of eating banana pudding, eat a banana. Instead of eating processed guacamole, eat the whole avocado. Consume things that are representative of the Wholeness, because your goal is Wholeness. Eat whole grain instead of (its components). The more that man has used his 'ingenuity' to tamper with Wholeness, the farther he's gotten away from Wholeness, which should only make sense. So to take that principle as it relates to food would mean take things the way that they came to you from nature. Try to cozy-up closer to (things in their) pristine state."**

> [Cathryn: *"But it won't prevent people being toxic physically,*

won't prevent people from getting through ... I mean it's important, but it won't prevent them from getting through?"] "Right, right. (It's just healthful). What I'm being shown is that there are qualitative levels of degree. It's not like you're either in Category A or you're in Category B. 'A' gets to go to this world and 'B' goes to this world. It's not like that. He's saying that there are gradations of quality of the experience. It's like when you're experiencing your last life. If you have a knowingness of this and you've been preparing yourself for it, you're going to have a deeper appreciation of what you're able to experience as you're going through (the Passage). So there are gradations of the quality of the experience when going through the Passage."

THE FATE OF THOSE WHO DO NOT BELIEVE IN REINCARNATION

Cathryn posed the question as to what happens to those who don't believe in reincarnation. It's a logical question to ask. After all, how could one possibly be prepared to experience a review of one's past life experiences if they didn't believe in reincarnation in the first place? What followed was my attempt to give an explanation using a story I had heard while I was a student at MIU (Maharishi International University) in 1979.

[Cathryn: "Those who don't believe in past lives. What happens to them?"] "(I remember a story where) there was a lawsuit where the TM (Transcendental Meditation) movement was sued because they were trying to get (their teachings) into the public school system, saying 'It's not a religion.' So this man who was a former TM teacher sued them, saying, 'It's a lie. I know what their secrets are because I was trained to be (one of their teachers). This really is a religion masquerading as something not religious (but scientific).' And (I was told a story while at MIU where) Charlie Lutes (a early participant in the TM movement and a frequent lecturer) was one of the ones called to testify. (As it turned out) he did not help the Movement's cause because he was extraordinarily frank. And (one of the attorneys for the plaintiff) said, 'Isn't it true that you people believe in reincarnation . . . you're going to eventually take another (physical) form. You're going to come back again.' (He may have been) expecting Charlie Lutes to deny it. But Charlie replied, 'Yes, that's absolutely what we say — and that's what you're going to believe, too, about 20 seconds after you kick off.' (or something to that effect).

The reason I'm telling you this story is because I think there may be this point when we go through the Passage where people will be allowed to see — if their heart is just opened a little bit — as I did on our April 10th session, 'Oh my God! . . . What I have been!' Ultimately reincarnation is not something that you 'believe' in. You don't own the knowledge if it's an article of faith. It is something you accept because you've had intimate experiences with your own distant past, as I have. It is something that everyone can and should experience."

[Cathryn: "And we've incarnated on other planets and in other forms?"] "Well, I'm including all of that. I'm not saying that all of that was on this planet. I was in shock as to the experience of it. I don't know if it was some of those other parallel universes. I don't know the mechanics of how this works. I'm not sure that either of us is going to know all the (small details prior to Passage). I think it is enough (to present) the broad picture that people are going to understand the importance of preparing. Then the answers to all our questions will be something that we'll (all) know when we're in Fullness."

[Cathryn: "So when we go through the Passage to get to the other side, are we still going to have our physical bodies or are we going to be in 'light bodies?'"] "We'll still be in physical bodies, but they'll have a very unique quality to them that we don't really understand now. Because bodies as they are physically, as they are perceived by others and how you perceive your own body, those things will change. What I'm being shown is that the perception of physicality is supported by a certain foundation of the ambient energies that exist for both the perceiver and the perceived. If the energetic situation changes then the perceptual assumptions and experiences will change, as well."

WHY HE DOESN'T MAKE HIMSELF MORE MANIFEST

As the reader may have observed from previous sessions, not all questions during the sessions were posed by Jack or Cathryn. At times I would ask questions myself and then wait for an answer. At one point I became frustrated because I felt that if I were being used as a conduit by the Divine to issue forth such an important message, I should be experiencing much more of the unfoldment for myself — particularly when I'm in my ordinary, waking state of consciousness.

[I directed my thought directed toward God: "Why don't you make yourself more manifest?" "I'm asking: 'Why don't I feel more the unfolding for myself? And why do I have to take ayahuasca to experience this?"] **"And the reply was: 'He wants us to try. He wants us to put a little effort into it. He gives enough that we can know the fabric of Creation, so we can know where we came from, what our purpose is, where our Bliss will be, and He wants us to make an effort. He doesn't want to just drop it in our lap. He wants us to make an effort to reach the finish line. In a sense, the circle would not be complete if it was just presented to us. God wants us to love Him back and it wouldn't work if we didn't use our free will to get to that. He's not going to force us to love Him. We've been through that: it's something we covered in a previous session. He's saying, there has to be a willful effort on our part to get there. And if He manifests Himself, if He sends His angels, if He produces miracles for us; then it makes it easy for us to the point where it's not (an act of love on our part). It's easy enough for Him to do, but then it's like, 'Where is your effort? If I make Myself manifest the way you want Me to then where is the effort on your part? Because if I gave you a fraction of what I'm capable of then you'd be 'wowed' by that and then where is your effort?'**

"He's saying part of the process is of Him appearing or feeling like (as if) He's absent from our lives. (Which creates) this void that we feel in our hearts. (And) He wants us to use our effort to fill that void with His Love."

THE IMPORTANT ROLE OF CO-CREATION

"Our role is very important in terms of Co-creation. We're on the receiving end of this Love, and we are on the vanguard of Creation's return to itself. (Nonetheless) we still have to use our will to imagine what life could be and should be, which He understands is difficult because (the world's) such a mess right now. But still, our thoughts co-create what happens in the future. It's always been that way and just because this Event is upon us doesn't change that fact. We have to make the effort to use our thoughts to co-create what we move into. I can tell that He feels this enormous pain that I'm in right now — with our lives (and world) collapsing on so many

levels. So He's saying, 'Still . . . still it is important that (with) whatever life is left within you that (you) make the effort to co-create into the unfoldment.'"

NEW MEANING FOR THE LORD'S PRAYER

At one point early in the April 28th session, I was surprised to encounter an angelic presence who brought up the "Lord's Prayer" as having a renewed significance in terms of the Passage and Split:

"One angelic being is telling me that The Lord's Prayer has meanings at different frequencies, and different levels of consciousness. Saying it and understanding its meaning has a kind of honing effect of its own." It's an interesting communication:

"Our Father Who art in Heaven — hallowed be Your Name." God resides in Wholeness. It is a state of consciousness. His 'name' or consciousness is hallowed because out of that state of consciousness the entirety of Creation unfolds.

"Thy Kingdom come, they will be done — on Earth as it is in Heaven." The Kingdom is the Singularity. In that state of Unity everything operates within the will of the Divine, because all souls within the Singularity are attuned to Him. This line only gains true meaning within the Singularity, because if we look at the state of earth, where is there any evidence that things are being 'done' in accordance with the will of the Divine? There isn't. Anti-Singularity rules. On the New Earth — the Kingdom — God's will prevails because earth and heaven are within the Singularity, and people live in Unity within the consciousness of God.

"Give us this day our daily bread." Whether one gathers their nourishment from the vegetables in their garden or the rarified energy of the ether, in Unity Consciousness there is always conscious awareness that all sustenance comes from the Divine. Asking God for sustenance (as this line is an imperative) signifies that we are asking for the means to return His Love back into Creation.

"And forgive us our trespasses as we forgive those who trespass against us." This line only reaches its fullest meaning in the Singularity, where any perceived slight between two parties is recognized as coming out of the Wholeness. True forgiveness from the heart only emanates from one who is enlightened and sees all other souls as manifestations of his own *true self*. Its invocation is an act of co-creation — to enable a life of Unified consciousness within an enlightened society.

"But lead us not into temptation, and deliver us from Evil, — Amen." The closing of the Lord's Prayer is a heartfelt request to avoid those conditions which would exclude the soul from Unity, or distance one from God's Grace. It reaches the pinnacle of its intended meaning in a positive outcome with the Passage, where one joins other souls on the New Earth, avoiding the exclusion from the Singularity that is the come for the 'Old.' An updated translation of this line might read, "Lead us not into the temptations and attachments that would keep us tethered to the old earth, and deliver us permanently from evil by helping us co-create with you, Oh Lord, a New Earth — a life of eternal Unity with You! Amen!"

"Why, who makes much of a miracle?
As to me I know of nothing else but miracles . . .

To me every hour of the light and dark is a
 miracle,
Every cubic inch of space is a miracle,
Every square yard of the surface of the earth is
 spread with the same,
Every foot of the interior swarms with the same.
To me the sea is a continual miracle,
The fishes that swim—the rocks—the motion of
 the waves—the ships with men in them,
What stranger miracles are there?"

~ Walt Whitman — "Miracles"

Chapter 10:

Conclusion

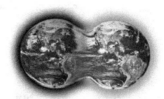

I have chosen to entitle the closing chapter of the "Message" section of this book "Conclusion," fully admitting that the *revelations* are a "work in progress." As we approach the middle of May, each journey breaks through a new threshold in my understanding of the "unfoldment" or to use the "focusing telescope" metaphor, a new adjustment towards clarity in what the Gospel of 2012 really means. I do not doubt that this image will only attain to a sharp, crystal clear resolution when we have made it to the end of 2012.

At each stage of the process — between conducting vision quests, transcribing recordings, and adding new chapters — I have had to confront the limits of my own frailty, prejudices (because we all have them), and skepticism. The overpowering influence of my "relativistic mind" is as strong as anyone's. Never in my wildest dreams did I ever imagine I would be involved in such work. It is a radical departure from anything else I've ever done in my life, and as I have stated repeatedly throughout the text — it will remain a mystery until I have fully integrated everything I have experienced why I would have been chosen for such a project.

Nevertheless, now that you have some inkling of the immense possibilities that await us as we approach the Passage — however this event manifests for each of us. The most important question is; What will you do about it? If you are like me, there are serious questions that remain, and if there is anything in the text itself which elicits, "This is unbelievable," you are in good company. However, if I have managed to accomplish anything at all with you, I certainly hope that it is the kindling of a desire on your part to "own your own truth." I have been told repeatedly that as we approach the Singularity, we will have the opportunity to communicate with the Divine through the *opening in the heart* so that we can obtain our own "direct connection" to reality.

In this sense we are *all* chosen. The Divine wants all of us to take our "vision quests" seriously — no matter what material aids from nature you use (or don't use) in your effort to resolve this yearning we have all felt for so long. And my belief is that in moments unexpected, you will find (as I have) these unanticipated "clues" that will point you in the right direction. The more energy you put into the search, you more you will attract the answers that will bring you home.

This very morning before breakfast, I was standing on my porch, communing with the clouds above — a practice I had seen my mother do so many times. Suddenly I was overcome with sensations that I realized I had never experienced before. At first I thought I was feeling a "frozen moment"— that deep silence that exists between each note within the symphony that is a human life. . . but no, this was something more. As I used my heart to settle in deeper to what this sensation might be, I realized that I was experiencing a narrowing of the "ley lines" or "magnetic flux"[1] in the time-space continuum. I can't think of any other words to describe it. Like the grain of sand in the hour glass, I was feeling the pull of the vortex that will eventually take all of us out of the "upper globe" and into "time past." I was feeling the speeding up of events, the accelerated global chaos born of frantic desperation emanating from the Anti-Singularity — and in that very moment I heard one of my spirit guides whisper in my ear with unusual solemnity: *"Hold onto the reins ... It's already started."*

I have no doubt that you, too, will experience something very similar in the weeks and months to come. But still . . . how will you perceive your experience, as a spectator or participant? As one who leaves fate to chance or as one who has accepted the Divine Invitation to help forge a New World?

And this *is* the promise of the Singularity: a New World — a state of interconnectedness where the true happiness of one demands the happiness of all, where the ebb and flow of life is *experienced* as never-ending waves of Love and Bliss — that same clay in the hands of the potter that set Creation into motion. Not as a conjecture, a philosophy, a system, a creed, a belief, a faith, some therapeutic healing balm to treat the wounded soul that feels it can't stand one more day in an unspeakably corrupt world. Not as something to be thought about — but something to be lived. This is the state of knowingness that transcends all teachings, all spiritual practices, and the perverting influences of eons of propagandistic fog that filled the vacuum that was created when we forgot who we were, where we came from, and the intense Love and Affection from whence we were conceived.

The return Home is not automatic. It will require some effort, and

---

1   See Wikipedia: (https://en.wikipedia.org/wiki/Ley_lines and https://en.wikipedia.org/wiki/Magnetic_flux)

we have so little time to get it right — a mere matter of months. But it is more than possible . . . in fact we should feel that it is inevitable. Having fallen off the ship of Divine Love and hopelessly, frantically, struggled in the cold ocean water below for countless lives, we are finally being thrown a lifeline. All we have to do is grab it and hold on for dear life. How tragic it would be if we missed the opportunity to grab that line . . . before our ship sails off into the horizon . . . never to be seen again.

In the session of May 2nd, I asked the Divine to (let me) *experience on the level of heart,* in a more intimate way, what life would feel like on the New Earth. I needed to experience emotionally what it felt like to be there. It was the last in a series of pleadings to tether myself to an existence I was allowed to channel, but which my ever-nagging intellect told me was too good to be true.

In an instant I was transported to the most spectacular garden I had ever seen — on this planet or any of the other worlds I have been privileged to visit. I saw strange structures, geometric shapes and symbols that strangely appeared to have been created to make the plants happier. The experience of communication between people, animals, plants — with everything in one's environ was experienced as the passage of thought within a unified whole. I immediately noticed that in something so ordinary as the movement of a hand, arm, the turning of my head to look at something, the shift of my eyes from one charming plant to another — all beckoning me to give them attention — there was the experience of life as waves. Soft, gentle, loving waves — as if wadding through warm, shallow water and experiencing even the tiniest change in current, but infinitely less dense.

I could do nothing without feeling my *interconnectedness* with everything and everyone else around me. Every moment was magical, and every experience inspired awe. The joyfulness was incredibly intense. Even in the simple act of breathing in and out there was this rhythmic ebb and flow of love that produced a thrilling sensation I found most indescribable. The experience of having an unhappy moment seemed completely foreign to the very place itself. There was a beauty to my surroundings — between the gardens, animal paddocks, flowing brooks, bird feeders, simple thatched-roof dwellings — that words cannot describe. There was richness to life — everywhere and in every moment — that told me that there could be no other place in time or space that made me feel me more at home.

In fact, that was it. This *was Home.* This was where I was meant to be. This was what I had been searching for through millions of lives.

Only now I was experiencing the ultimate resolution to a search for which there could be no greater outcome. It was as if I had spent many millions of years trying to open a door with an unending series of keys that failed to budge the lock — and now finally, I was given the key that would spring the lock and allow me to open the door.

Naysayers may say that this is all a pipe dream. I'm sure there are those who feel that such experiences are only possible with the use of hallucinogens — not appreciating the irony that for those of us with extensive experience in the inter-dimensional realms, it is the return to this planet, in its current condition, that is the ultimate "bad trip." But even without so many entheogenic journeys, I can still *feel* what life can be, could be, and should be. I can *feel* the ultimate conclusion to My Purpose — a proper conclusion to which no substitute will do.

So, too, must *you feel the conclusion* to your journey . . . and accept no inferior substitute.

The Gospel of 2012 is your call to channel all of your pain, disgust, loneliness, dismay, and bewilderment into the fashioning of the Life Divine.

Life as you know it was meant to be lived.

Life as you know *you* were meant to live it.

You — and everyone else who hears the siren call of the Divine at this special time — are the *"strange attractors"* of chaos theory. You are that one perfectly-timed flutter of the butterfly's wing that has the power to completely reorder Creation.

As we proceed together towards the Passage and you intensify your "personal search," you will find that you are not alone. You will find that there are opportunities to network with other awakening hearts that can feel the same call. Synchronicities will guide you when you least expect them. Then you will find that an image of the New Earth is emerging not because it was sitting there waiting for you to *find* it . . . rather, it came into existence with the Love and Grace of a Creator — the long lost lover you never knew about — who has waited billions of years to get you back.

And together you *created* it.

Closing Thought: In light of the quickly changing circumstances we can all expect to see, particularly in the last half of 2012; we have created a website to help keep you updated on new visions, Live Webinars (with questions/answers), Nexus Points (with a comments section), confirming world events, and an archive of audio clips (pre-book and recent journeys). If you are not already a Member, go to www.Gospel2012.com/join-register and register now.

Book Two
Nexus Points

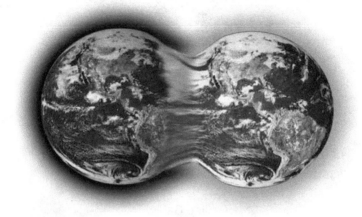

"One cannot enter don Juan's world intellectually, like a dilettante seeking fast and fleeting knowledge. Nor, in don Juan's world, can anything be verified absolutely. The only thing we can do is arrive at a state of increased awareness that allows us to perceive the world around us in a more inclusive manner."

~ Carlos Castenada

"All truths are easy to understand once they are discovered; the point is to discover them."

~ Galileo Galilei

In Search of the Nexus Points

As I discussed in the Introduction, from the very first reading I received concerning 2012, in November, 2011, validity was a pressing issue. It wasn't that the information provided didn't seem authentic. On the contrary, these vision quests were, by far, the most profound spiritual experiences I've ever had in my life. Nonetheless, the information provided was so astonishing and the implications so mind-boggling that at times I felt mentally numb at the end of a session.

In the Introduction, I also referenced my November 11th, 2006 vision quest wherein I first made telepathic contact with the ayahuasca plant spirit — something that nearly all ayahuasqueros experience early in their calling. It was during this session that I was told that I would be instrumental in doing something that would "help change the world." There was an air of Divine appointment in the communication, one which I find almost impossible to communicate. I was shocked, humbled, and overwhelmed in a way where words simply fail to convey the intensity of the experience. Instantly, the thought arose within me, "I'm not worthy to do this," and the reply was just as instantaneous — with an unmistakable, chastising tone, "This isn't about you. This isn't about worthiness. It's about destiny."

It wasn't until sometime in March, 2012, when I was told in one of the sessions to compose a book that contains the information you've been reading, that it really hit me. Although I was given the first snippet of information in November (2011), concerning the Passage, it would take five months for me to make the relevant connection to what I was told back in 2006. There was a point where each session seemed increasingly more difficult. As the revelations grew in intensity, I found a growing, countermanding force arise within me. At no point, regardless of what was communicated, was I very far away from my nagging doubts or skeptical nature. Every message grew in its ability to affront countless scientific, mathematical, and empirical principles and observations that formed the clue that held my view of reality together. On several occasions in the mornings following a session, I would end up telling Cathryn over breakfast, **"Either the information that's being conveyed to me is the most phenomenal in the history of Mankind, or I must be severely psychotic."**

The internal conflict reached a breaking point in the April 10th journey — the details of which form the chapter entitled, "Awakening." After this session, I had fully intended to prevent any of its particulars from entering this book. Not only did the events stretch credulity, but the personal aspects of the journey were just so embarrassing. It was only after I began this chapter that I realized that it had a place in beginning our discussion of nexus points. I want the reader to know that despite the extreme profundity of all I have experienced, I have still found the need to find supportive external "signs" that would help me fit the pieces of the puzzle together.

I made a decision shortly after I was "told" to write this book that I was going to include a Nexus Point section. I was told that it was going to become increasingly important to look out for "synchronicities" as I proceeded on my path as early as the 2004, when I was imprisoned in Lafayette, Louisiana. (The extraordinary experiences connected with this revelation is the subject of Chapter 3 of *Meditopia®* — a free read online at www.meditopia.org.[1] The relevant section was authored prior to my re-imprisonment in Texas in September, 2004). So it's important for the reader to know that I would have sought out instances of 'divine coincidence' for my own benefit, even if they weren't of value for the reader.

Below, you will find recent a series of revelations and synchronicities, which taken together as a whole, provide more "insights from unrelated sources." Each "nexus point" makes one or more references — either directly or in passing — to events which were detailed previously. (For those "nexus points" that involve video, we provide instructions below on how to find the relevant information, or you can log onto "www. Gospel2012.com." Additional thought-provoking nexus points can be found on the website, as well. Remember, the value is not in what is conveyed in any one point. It is the total picture that is our goal.) You may think of this exercise the way you would examining the spokes of a wheel. Each spoke sees the hub from a different angle, and yet it is the totality of the spokes that support and uphold the uniform, equidistant relationship between the hub and the wheel.

Let's begin.

---

1   A recounting of my false imprisonment begins at: (http://meditopia.org/chap3-3.htm)

Biblical References / Christian Mystics

There are numerous biblical references to a period of "three days of darkness," and, in fact, it appears to be a permanent fixture of Christian eschatology.[2] Although interpretations vary greatly, near all references to the "three days of darkness" are in connection to a return of Christ and a defeat of evil.

Synchronicity:

The reference to an "end time" period of three days of darkness can be found in many religious traditions, but it is especially accentuated in Christian tradition. At the time of the first reading where this reference was made, I immediately recognized the similarity between the description of this event and my Christian upbringing. Moreover, I find it interesting that where Christians refer to an "end time," the reference is not far from this, namely, "an end of time as you know it." The other unmistakable similarity is that Christian eschatology — in any of its variations — describes this "end time" as involving an event where goodness triumphs and evil is defeated.

Notable Points of Difference or Omission:

In all of the revelations that form the very substance of this book, never was there any hint of bias to one particular religious tradition. There is no mention of a return of any particular personality, something fundamental to so many of the world's religious teachings and indigenous prophesies. There is no mention of a Messiah. There is only one constant refrain that the end of 2012 is about a return to one, absolute, indivisible God, who is the basis for all Creation, and that his message transcends any and all intermediaries, including this author. Additionally, the eschatological reference to "three days of darkness" has been mentioned by countless Christian mystics, and although social conditions marking its imminence have been described, no definitive date has been agreed upon in the over 2,000 years since these prophesies first began to surface.

Terence McKenna

My first exposure to Terence's work came in the 2005, when I read two of his seminal works while imprisoned in Texas.[3] Although Terence

---

2   Eschatology please see: (https://en.wikipedia.org/wiki/Eschatology); see Joel 2:10, 31; Isaiah 13:10 and 24:23; Zechariah 14:6,7; Matthew 24:25,29; Mark 13:24; Luke 21:25; Acts 2:19,20; Revelation 6:12,14; 8:2. Also see: (https://en.wikipedia.org/wiki/Three_Days_of_Darkness). A good online summary begins at: (https://www.abovetopsecret.com/forum/thread794416/pg1)

3   The two works by McKenna cited are: *The Invisible Landscape: Mind, Hallucinogens, and the I Ching*; and *The Archaic Revival*.

initially gave no exact date in his initial work concerning what would occur in 2012, he steadily maintained from the mid-70's until his death in 2000 that using his concept of "Timewave Zero," the closing of 2012 would bring "a singularity of infinite complexity," marking the end of time as we know it.

Synchronicity:

The "Passage" is noted in several of my sessions as an "end of time as we know it and understand it." McKenna's characterization of the end of 2012 as a time when "anything and everything imaginable will occur simultaneously" seems to correlate with the phenomenon of masses of people coalescing with parts of themselves from other parallel universes — which collapse into a unified whole, combined with present life, past life, and collective life "reviews." The entire message of this book as it relates to the "Passage" closely resonates with the ambiguous description of "singularity" that was McKenna's most poignant trademark. Additionally, the use of ayahuasca as practiced by the indigenous people's of the Western Amazon is a common feature of both McKenna and this author.

Notable Points of Difference or Omission

McKenna never appeared to connect the ending of 2012 to anything astrophysical. Moreover, although McKenna felt that this would be a time of enormous spiritual significance, he never provided the kind of detail that was the basis for my publishing the present work.

Princess Nakamaru

As a speaker at the Pythagoras Conference 2012,[4] Ms. Nakamaru makes the claim that some time in the 1970's, her spiritual "third eye" was opened which has subsequently allowed her to communicate with ET's and underground civilizations, travel psychically, and have certain knowledge of the future.[5]

Synchronicity

Nakamaru is also clear on the major points involving how 2012 ends which are strikingly similar to what has been revealed in this book. These points of commonality include:

• The three days of darkness at the end of 2012, following

---

4   Pythagoras Conference — See http://www.pythagorasconferenceglobal.com. There are many YouTube videos now that cover Nakamaru's experiences and perspective.
5   See http://www.youtube.com/watch?v=LpHt1Vr_40Y, http://www.youtube.com/watch?v=ucC4HKaTQOw, or the longer official video presentation from the Conference at: http://www.youtube.com/watch?v=RysTa60GBcg.

December 22nd,

- the failure of electricity during his time,

- we must "purify ourselves spiritually" in preparation for this event,

- the existence of another earth-like planet which evolves from this,

- the knowledge of a Global Elite that know this is going to happen and are keeping it from the Masses,

- that their preparations will not save them because the changes that need to be made in preparation for the Passage are spiritual.

Notable Points of Difference or Omission

Nakamaru talks about ascending to the Fifth Dimension, whereas the material herein speaks of a kind of "merging" of the third, fourth, and fifth dimensions perceptually. Although Nakamaru talks about another world, she does not — in the videos footnoted here — or in her other discussions online, describe a splitting of the Earth.

Dolores Cannon

I was already familiar with some of Dolores's work, as a good friend was involved in a publishing project with Dolores involving reported communications with Nostradamus years earlier. (The resulting three volume work was entitled, *"Conversations with Nostradamus."*) It was only in February, 2012, that a friend told me about some striking similarities between what I was being told and what Delores was reporting through psychic channeling.[6]

Synchronicity

In a montage of different YouTube videos, Dolores describes the end of 2012 as involving the creation of a New Earth that comes out of the current Earth.

This has never happened anywhere in the universe — namely, the movement of an entire planet into a new dimension. The New Earth will be completely "new and beautiful." Those who go to the New Earth are those who have prepared, raising their vibrations to the requisite level.

---

6   See Dolores' interview at http://www.youtube.com/watch?v=YUmHxCDAuS8, or go to http://3MagicWordsMovie.com. Also, see http://in5d.com.

Preparation is added by avoiding "heavy foods" like red meat, and opting instead for fresh whole fruits and vegetables, what she calls "lighter foods."

Those who remain on the Old Earth "will stay with what they have created . . . not everyone can change their vibration that quickly." They will have to deal with the negativity of all those left behind. She equates the Biblical passage (Book of Revelations) concerning "The New Heaven and the New Earth" to the emerging New Earth.

Dolores talks about "those in the middle" as being the focus concerning those who "can be saved." This mimics the session I had that described a kind of spiritual triage where more attention was being given to those viewed as ready to make the ascension.

Dolores indicates that she was at a conference with Annie Kirkwood (author of *Mary's Message to the World*), who described the Split as the earth going through cellular mitosis and dividing into two earths. This is a spot-on match for exactly what I was shown, in every detail.

As in my own sessions, Dolores says she has been told that the really disastrous earth changes occur with the Old Earth, as will even more serious wars. This occurs after the Split. Populated by peoples who love their negativity, a disastrous future on the earth's surface is their inheritance as "they work out their karma."

She sees the end of 2012 as the time that has been designed to "make the shift." Moreover, the event cannot be changed. "It's too late to turn back now."

Dolores is not without influence from the Mayan meme. "The Mayans foresaw this as the biggest event to ever happen in history. What's about to happen has never happened before in the history of the Universe."

Notable Points of Difference or Omission

A good deal is said about raising one's vibration in preparation for the New Earth, but the development of the heart and any mention of feeling Love from the Creator is absent — at least in the materials I reviewed. Additionally, graduating to the New Earth is said to be about graduating to the fifth dimension, a similar view portrayed by Princess Nakamaru. Dolores says that with additional time our physical bodies will become "bodies of light." This differs from life on the New Earth as it was shown to me.

Pane "Astral Walker" Andov

The following comes from a Nexus Magazine conference in

Queensland, Australia (July 23-25, 2011), during which Pane Andov gave a lecture entitled, "Cosmic Coincidences and Expectations for 2012."[7]

Andov, an regular ET contactee since the age of 7, is a teacher of astral projection, kundalini yoga, and various other yogic disciplines. In 1995-96, Andov was told that "there would be an extraordinary cosmic event in 2012." Much later, in 2008, Andov was shown a "holographic projection" of what would happen around December 23, 2012. It involves enormous energy coming from the galactic center which has the power to transform a large number of humans. "Humanity is heading towards a great change, many spirits will return to the stars and something magnificent is going to happen."

Andov later founded a magazine entitled, *Sixth Sense*, which covers many arcane mystical subjects, including genuine crop circles, of which "over 20,000" have been cited worldwide over the past few decades. Andov claims these are directed from benevolent ET species who are disturbed because "our governments are deceiving us. They are not providing us the real situation on the planet, the real situation in the Milky Way (galaxy); what we really are and what are potential are [sic]." He notes efforts that governments and various military agencies have made to discredit the crop circle phenomenon, the intent of whose designers is to impart information to humanity that might otherwise be inaccessible. One example is the creation of man-made crop circles, which are messy operations — never the precise, clean, message-imbued images that are part and parcel of "genuine" crop circles.

Andov poses the question, "What are the crop circles saying about 2012?" The short explanation is that "there is a gate, a portal, at the center of the Milky Way galaxy . . . there is a hole and an explosion." This phenomenon causes enormous energy to be sent along the galactic plane "to the edges of the galaxy. It is a wave coming from the galactic center." Andov points to the significance of the July, 2008 crop circle at Avebury Manor, England,[8] which clearly shows all the planets of our solar system as they would appear on Sunday, December 23, 2012 — (the only small anomaly being the position of Pluto, a planet smaller than our moon, which Andov explains). An enormous hologram that appeared over Christchurch, New Zealand, in March 29, 2011 also replicated the communication that December 23, 2012 is hugely significant. Subsequent crop circle activity has communicated that the energy

---

7   Pane's lecture at the Nexus Conference can be seen at (http://www.youtube.com/watch?v=1q2Du_DkKbo). Additional information can be found at (http://www.paneandov2012.com).

8   See Crop Circle Connector website (http://www.cropcircleconnector.com/anasazi/time2011c.html)

approaching from the center of the Milky Way will begin to be observable in the sky on December 13, 2012.

Andov points to several crop circles showing a snake looping back and devouring its own tail. "The completion of a circle." Additionally, he emphasizes the spiritual implications of these astrophysical events. "We need to remember who we are. We are infinite consciousness—cosmic consciousness — that is having a human experience. We are Light beings." He claims we are only using 3% of the capability of our genetic material, but this will change radically as a result of the events that are coming at the end of the year. The cultivation of love and the development of the heart play a role in preparing for what's about to happen. "We need to change our vibrational level. We have to stop killing animals, fish, and birds, because when we consume these, we are absorbing the vibrational effects of the violence that occurred in their slaughter."

Incredibly, Andov was told that the Event brings with it higher vibrational frequencies so that we can know who we were in our previous incarnations and "how the Universe works. All our genetic material will be recovered . . . The game is over. We are all free."

Andov makes clear that this result is not automatic. "Currently many ET's are leaving the Earth because they realize that time is running out and the positive side is losing."

Andov closes with "ET Ultimate Message for Humanity," which he summates, "This can end in two ways. One way, we can produce Heaven on Earth. The other, everything will go to pieces and Humanity will have to repeat the cycle. If we learn our lessons we will be okay, but if we don't the life of planet earth will be erased. Period. There is a way to change the outcome, and the message of that is the only reason those crop circles have been appearing. And the ultimate message is that this is something that needs to be created in every aura (done throughout to affect things on the planetary level)." The flower of life yantra contains the vibration related to the rebirth — (and, in fact, Andov conducts Flower of Life meditations from Australia every Sunday).

Additionally, the innate intelligence behind the energy that is coming is emphasized. "It will scan you to the bone. It can tell if you are ready for the transition or not. There is no fooling it."

Synchronicity

The coincidences are innumerable. The cosmic event involving the galactic center and its timing, one that has never happened here before. The Divine intelligence that appears to be behind it. Its profound effect on human consciousness. Our divine responsibility and the importance of preparation. The fact that the positive side is losing, inferring that not many are going to make it. The ability to have all our genetic material combined — (marriage with all our soul fragments?) — our ability to see all our past lives and understand how the Universe works. The fact that governments worldwide have worked to suppress the information they have about this astrophysical event.

Notable Points of Difference or Omission

Andov goes into detail on ET revelations concerning a rapid expansion of the sun that will occur between December 23, 2012 and March 28, 2013. This event will bring about extreme heat on the earth's surface and is the real reason that so many Western national governments have invested trillions of dollars in the aggregate building huge underground cities. They have enough food, water, and other provisions for members of the Elite to live underground for 5 years. Nowhere is such an event mentioned in my sessions, and it would appear that if this event does unfold, it will occur within the realm of the Old Earth.

As a precursor to the stream of energy that will hit earth from the galactic center, Andov recounts the findings of NASA's Ibex satellite, which has found an interspacial "ribbon" that is millions of degrees C., and highly magnetic, into which our Solar System will be moving later this year. This process, Andov says, will initiate a process by which the sun is accelerated on its path to becoming first a "red giant" and then a "white dwarf." Nothing related to this was communicated to me, either.

One glaring omission is that nowhere does Andov mention a *splitting* of the earth. To hear him tell it, a positive outcome sounds like an "all or nothing event." This doesn't comport with my communication. We are NOT all in this together. The destiny of those who are taken to the New Earth is nothing like that of those who are forced to remain, for lack of preparation.

Don Alejandro — Mayan Shaman[9]

The predictions of Don Alejandro of the Mayan Council in Guatemala are a reflection of the common interpretation of Mayan elders who have stood guard over the Mayan teachings, primarily through oral tradition, for centuries. Essentially, it is a time of spiritual rebirth. We are about exit the fourth sun and enter the fifth. There is nothing to be afraid of, as it has happened many times before.

---

9 A good summation about Don Alejandro's view and advice concerning 2012. See (www. youtube.com/watch?v=wbAvF0Qcb2o, also see www.mayanmajix.com)

Synchronicity

The primary correlation has to do with the spiritual significance of what happens at the end of this year. I was told very much the same thing when I spoke with Grandfather Martin of the Hopi tribe in 2007.

Notable Points of Difference or Omission

What has been communicated to me is that what we experience at the end of this year has never happened before. It may be the end of a cycle, yes — but a much larger one than is portrayed in the various indigenous prophesies I have read or heard about. The general advice, "Don't worry. Be happy," does not comport with what is communicated to me, either. Preparation is key to get the most from what we are about to experience — and that's an understatement.

The Strange Case of Robert D. Wilkins

On September 24, 2004, I self-reported to U.S. federal authorities after being handed a 33 month prison sentence for supposed violations of FDA law. (Again — for those that are interested — the coerced plea agreement, efforts by federal agents to fleece my wife and I of whatever assets we had, and related skullduggery that led to this event, as well as my decision to leave the U.S. and never return, is the subject of Chapter 3 of *Meditopia*®).

I spent the next month in the oh-so-loving care of authorities at Calcasieu Parish Correctional Center in Lake Charles, Lousiana, (known as "CCC"), before being transferred to the Federal Correctional Center in Beaumont, Texas. However, before being admitted to "general population," I had to endure three days in a concrete "holding cell," waiting to be processed. It was during this period that I spent time with Robert Wilkins — a self-confessed, long-term drug user, who was being charged with murder.

Many inmates are very reticent about talking once incarcerated. Nearly all criminal defense attorneys are firm and forthright in advising their clients not to discuss the pre-trial specifics of their case to other inmates — many of whom swarm over new arrivals, looking for the opportunity to pick up off-handed, incriminating statements. After all, the testimony of informants — whether true or false, it doesn't matter — is the lifeblood of prosecutors, who care little about the veracity of such statements, as long as it will help secure a conviction. "Snitches" — for their part — are highly motivated to spin eye-popping yarn, because cooperation in providing even fabricated testimony can mean years off an otherwise draconian prison sentence.

Though Robert — then 28 — would wait more than seven more years at CCC before going to trial, I found his frankness, in discussing not only the specifics of his case but his life leading up to it, quite unusual. (Robert was later convicted of killing "Tony" Fontenot in January, 2012. He was formally sentenced the following month to a life sentence and today resides at the Louisiana State Penitentiary in Angola, Louisiana.)

Besides telling me that he had stabbed his drug dealer with a knife after his supplier caught up with him, demanding that he catch up on his account, he talked at length about his relationship with drugs. (Robert claims to have owed Tony more than $5,000 for his drugs and was told on the evening of the dispute that if he didn't come up with the money, Tony would kill him. In a provincial, Southern, racially charged town like Lake Charles, some would suggest that Robert being white and the victim being black only aggravated the circumstances.)

"I've been a drug addict for many years now," Robert told me. "I've tried to quit, but I just can't . . . but the unusual thing is that over the years I've acquired certain abilities that have I wouldn't have had otherwise."

I initially found this to be a dubious claim. Lake Charles is a hotbed of recreational drug abuse — marijuana, meth, cocaine, crack, OxyContin — and so much more. The ascending status of the area as a gambling mecca over the past twenty years has only made matters worse, not to mention the stressful, debilitating effects of industry, as Calcasieu Parish contains one of the highest concentrations of toxic, ever-polluting, petrochemical plants to be found anywhere in the world. And yet . . . in the 23 years I lived in the area, not once had I ever heard the claim that a recreational drug provided anyone with any other ability besides "getting high."

Nonetheless, Robert had such a candid quality to him that I couldn't help but inquire further.

"Ok, what ability do you think you have now that you wouldn't have had if you hadn't abused drugs?"

Robert told me that he had problems keeping girlfriends, because it was all too easy to "freak them out." An example he gave me was the ability to hear the telephone and from the sound of the ring tell who was calling and what their intention was. "A girlfriend isn't prepared to hear, 'Pick up the phone, baby. Your mother's calling and she wants to know if we're still coming over for dinner tomorrow night.'" I had a tough time discounting this, because, at times, my own mother was able to pick up unusual tidbits from the sound of the telephone.

"Okay, well . . . what other unusual abilities have you picked up over the years?" I inquired.

"I can see the future," he stated matter-of-factly. "I don't control what I see or when I'll see it, but the imagery is more real than everyday life. When I'm in this certain state, everything is more real than 'life' — colors are richer and deeper, sounds are sharper and more distinct, all the senses are amplified."

"Can you give me an example?" I asked. "Pick what you think is the most incredible experience you've ever had about a future event."

"Well," he thought for a moment. "There was this time around 1997 when I was in an altered state and I found myself walking through Central Park in New York. It was a calm day, everything around me was serene, and then all of a sudden I see this incredibly bright light to my left. I mean incredibly bright — like you can't imagine. I thought maybe New York was being hit by a nuclear weapon or something. There is chaos everywhere, people screaming . . . and then all of a sudden everything stops. Time stops. And then everything, everything goes to pitch black. It isn't black as you know it. It's total darkness like nothing you've ever experienced. And then out of this incredible darkness I see this image in white and it says, '2012.'"

"So that's it? . . . That was your experience?" I asked, slightly irritated, thinking that Robert had heard about the Mayan prophesies concerning 2012 and was simply dressing it up and putting his own spin on it.

"Yeah . . ."

"So this is your way of telling me that this is your take on the Mayan prophesies about 2012, right?"

"Mayan what? . . . I have no idea what you're talking about."

For the next 20 minutes I continued to talk to Robert about the prophesies, what various people thought they meant, and what other people thought was the significance of the year 2012. At the conclusion of our talk I came to the conclusion that Robert really didn't know anything about the prophesies. He didn't read much, nor did he have any personal knowledge or orientation as it related to anything eschatological. He knew nothing about the Mayans, nor did the year 2012 carry any significance to him. It was just another year, as far as he was concerned. In actuality, Robert was everything he said he was: a tormented soul who'd had a tough life, a history of involvement with illegal drugs, who had now gotten himself into serious trouble because of a dispute turned lethal that he wished he'd never had.

Nearly four and a half years later, well after I moved to Ecuador with my family yet months before my illegal kidnapping, Cathryn wrote to Robert in prison. She recounted my experience of our conversation and in early 2009 received a reply from the States. On our website (in Nexus Points), you will find scans of two excerpts of his reply where Robert confirms the particulars I have described above — in his own handwriting.

Synchronicity

Wilkins was emphatic in his description of the "total darkness . . . like nothing you've ever experienced" that appeared before he was shown "2012." This is exactly how the "three days of darkness" was described to me. The chaos that results from what appears to be an explosion on the periphery of his vision intimates the global chaos that is being accelerated in 2012 from the Anti-Singularity.

The Even Stranger Case of Bill Wood aka William Brockbrader

There are a variety of excellent interviews of Bill Wood on the internet, the majority accessible from YouTube. The video referenced here, videotaped live in January, 2012, is a three part interview of Bill Wood by Kerry of the Camelot Project, wherein the three parts come to approximately 45 minutes in length.[10] Bill Wood relates his PSI experiences in working with highly classified military projects involving The Stargate Project, Yellow Cube, and Looking Glass. These projects involve efforts by the most powerful members of the Global Elite to foresee and control the future, alter time lines, even profit from securities trading. Bill does not flinch in telling his listeners that the things he has witnessed and done stretches the limits of what most people would be willing to accept. Ditto.

In late January Kerry Cassidy did a 3-hour interview with Bill Wood over Skype, which also included former partner Bill Ryan (see below) and David Wilcock.[11] Wood and Wilcock expanded upon their experiences/resources concerning various government projects involving a Singularity that the Elite know will occur at the end of 2012. David Wilcox claims to have vetted Bill Ryan and found his professional credentials and claims legitimate.

What makes this case so strange is not the revelations concerning known "end of 2012" phenomena, but rather the involvement of outside

---

10 The Bill Wood interview can be found on YouTube with Spanish subtitles: (http://www.youtube.com/watch?v=ICmWys6K2VA, or www.youtube.com/watch?v=pqOMP1gBPLo, www.youtube.com/watch?v=VO78waaYgs8)
11 See: www.youtube.com/watch?v=9k7JORWLFGo.

parties who have flooded online video sites and the blogosphere with accusations that Bill Woods was never a Navy SEAL and that his testimony should be questioned because of a military charge for sex with a sixteen-year-old girl that took place years prior when Bill was 25. I've gone through hours of online vitriol, and I've heard both sides of the arguments. I find both the criminal charge concerning Bill's involvement with an underage girlfriend, and the way that the SEAL community has attempted to portray Bill's military service as extremely fishy. I myself was a Navy cryptologist who held a Top Secret clearance in the 1970's, so I know a little bit about the environment. Nonetheless, irrespective of the circus acts that continue on the periphery, Bill's testimony is too valuable and too synchronous not to be included as a nexus point.

Synchronicity

Bill is very clear in portraying the Global Elite as very knowledgeable about events that will occur at the end of 2012. In fact, he indicates that even in the early 1990's, the Elite were referring to "The 2012 Problem." They know that they are on the losing side of a cosmic battle, but in their supreme arrogance, they still largely feel as a Group that they can outsmart the Forces that are behind the Event. Despite having first entered into this area through his work in military intelligence, he has come to the conclusion that the end of 2012 is "about spiritual Ascension." The framework he creates is shockingly similar to the revelations contained in this book.

Notable Points of Difference or Omission

Bill came to a point where he knew that his handlers in the Elite were scared to death of "the 2012 problem," but that neither he nor they could change "this thing that you don't wanna tell me about." There are no major differences here — only a lack of details, because remote viewing and similar psychic practices can only unearth certain broad details about the event.

Bill Ryan — Vilcabamba, Ecuador — January, 2012

In January I took a shuttle to Vilcabamba — a famous community in the province immediately south of us — with my friend, George Green.[12] George was scheduled to speak with several other lecturers

---

12 Vilcabamba was made popular after a January, 1973 article in National Geographic brought attention to its unusually high percentage of centenarians. It sits south of Loja, the capital of Ecuador's most southern mountain province which carries the same name — with Azuay Province to its north and the border with Peru to its south. As for George Green, he is a popular writer/lecturer on the coming collapse, having authored/channeled books such as *The New Paradigm*, *Becoming*, and *Messages for the Ground Crew*. His website is (www.nohoax.com.)

at a conference there, hosted by *Madre Tierra* ("Mother Earth"), a hotel/restaurant quite popular with local gringo residents as well as tourists. In fact, George and Bill Ryan — made famous by his work with the alternative, online, whistle-blower forum, "Project Camelot" — were the main speakers.[13]

While having lunch at Madre Tierra with George and Bill, I happened to mention some of the revelations concerning "the end of 2012" that had — up to that point — been revealed to me on my ayahuasca journeys. Little that I said appeared to resonate with Bill, who together with his former Camelot partner, Kerry, has interviewed scores of interesting subjects on a wide variety of alternative topics with widely varying opinions.

Almost as an aside, however, Bill recounted his experience with one German subject who claimed to be a member of the Illuminati with many connections at the highest levels of the global financial and political inner circle. In fact, Bill didn't reveal the name of this subject to me, who met privately with Bill and Kerry after insisting that he had something of great importance that they would want to hear.

As it turned out, the subsequent meeting turned out to be a source of considerable irritation for Bill. Not only was the subject not voluminous in what he had to report, but he insisted that the little he had to tell them was of supreme importance. As best as I can remember, here is how Bill described it:

"He told us that **the 'big secret' among the elite was that there was going to be three days of darkness at the end of this year.** This is widely known among the Elite who have no intention of letting it become commonplace knowledge among the masses. It is a big source of concern for them."

"That's it?" I asked.

"Well, that's the whole point. We went through a bit of trouble to interview this chap, and then this was all he had to tell us. When we asked him what else he could reveal, he declined, saying 'There's a lot more I could tell you. But I won't. I've told you enough, and now you know the big secret that the Elite doesn't want to have made public.' It was a real letdown."

Synchronicity

Self-explanatory.

13   See (www.projectcamelot.org.) If you enter "Project Camelot" into YouTube, you may be surprised at the sheer volume of uploads that pop up, or go to the dedicated YouTube channel, www.youtube.com/projectcamelot. Interestingly, Bill Ryan and Kerry Lynn Cassidy have recently ended their corroboration, with Kerry continuing with Project Camelot, while Bill — who now lives in Vilcabamba — continues with his own "Project Avalon.".

Ken Carey — December, 1978

At about the same time I had my first brahmic experience in Cobb Mountain, California — described earlier in Chapter 4 — Ken Carey was in bed with a cold and a high temperature. It was during this infirmity that Carey entered into a state of auditory hallucination — much like my own where there is no trance, no loss of consciousness, and no voice change — but obtained without the aid of an entheogen.

Carey found the information that was being communicated to him so profound and divinely inspired that he spent the next 11 days transcribing via typewriter what he had been told. Out of the experience and others subsequent to it, Carey wrote four books over the next eighteen years where he attempted to communicate the message and its importance to humanity.[14]

Although the timing of this cosmic event, "the first unified movement of the awakening planetary organism,"[15] is never pinpointed, his description of the event matches my own in innumerable ways. (As to timing, he seems initially attracted to the notion that it could be the end of the Mayan long count calendar, winter solstice of *2011*, which we now know to be a miscalculation.[16] Later on, in his final book, he declares that "the Earth has a due date sometime during the second decade of the twenty-first century.")[17]

But all issues of timing aside — because, in all fairness, I myself haven't been given an *exact* date and hour when the Passage will begin — the similarities in description appear more than coincidental.[18]

"There will be a great shift then, a single moment of Quantum Awakening. In this moment, the smallest interval of time measured in these dimensions — the interval that occurs in every atom between each of its billions of oscillations per second — will be lengthened unto infinity. An interval of non-time will expand. . ."

In several of the sessions, I was told outright, "This is the end of time (as you know and experience it)." That time would "expand" is an apt, though incomplete, description of the Passage. How else could one experience their past life, their previous incarnations, and a synopsis of the entire history of humanity unless three days were expanded into something considerably and experientially longer? This becomes clearer

---

14   These include: *The Starseed Transmissions: An Extra-Terrestrial Report*. Kansas City, Mo.: Uni-Sun, 1982; *Vision*. Kansas City, Mo.: Uni-Sun, 1985; *Starseed: The Third Millennium — Living in the Posthistoric World*. San Francisco: Harper, 1991.

15   Carey, *Starseed* (1991), p. 125.

16   Carey, *The Starseed Transmissions*, p. 22.

17   Carey, *Starseed* (1991), p. 125.

18   *Stray*, p. 197, 199 — references Carey, *Starseed*, p. 127.

in the next passage ...

- "Through that expansion eternity will flow. Some will experience this moment as minutes or hours, others as a lifetime. Still others will experience this flash of non-time as a succession of many lives, and some few will, in this moment, know the Nagual itself, the great nameless Presence that exists before and after all these worlds."

This excerpt supports the idea that the Passage is not only an opportunity to experience one's past fully, but that the experience will be vary from person to person. The greatest opportunity being offered is to experience and thereafter live in Unity Consciousness – to know "the great nameless Presence"... Source itself.

- "In the expanse of the non-time internal, human beings will have all the time they require to realize, experience, and remember fully consciousness of their eternal spirits, and to recall the origin of their individuality in the primordial fields of being."

The text of my sessions repeatedly contains references to understanding why God has done what he has done, going back to the very beginning. He wants us to *remember* ... everything. He want us to *understand* ... everything, going all the way back to the point of Creation, "the origin of individuality in the primordial fields of being." He wants us to have a relationship with Him that is so intimate that we stand inside "the Mind of God."

- "All will have ample time to recharge their form identity and its biological projection with the awareness of who they are, why they have individualized, and why they have chosen to associate with the planet's human expression. Each one will have the choice to return to biological form or to remain in the fields of disincarnate awareness."

The decision to remain or return to the New Earth is one of choice.

- "Those who choose to return to human form will do so, fully aware of who they are. No longer will they be but partially incarnate; they will resume biological residence with the full memory and consciousness of their eternal natures, sharing the creative capacities of the Star Maker, whose reflective cells they will then know themselves to be."

After attaining to the New Earth humans never lose their Unity

Consciousness. They share their "creative capacities" with the Creator — with whom they become co-creators.

> • Carey describes Mother Earth as having reproductive capacity after the "Quantum Awakening" (i.e. Passage), which uncannily parallels what I was told in connection with the Split between New and Old Earth.

Synchronicities

They are bountiful, and in certain parts of the text, with the substitution of certain proper nouns, you have a description of the same phenomenon. Interestingly, Carey refers to the event as "the Singularity" — as has Terrence McKenna. It is an expression that was "fed" to me as well, along with its evil twin, the "Anti-Singularity." As a matter of proper disclosure, I should inform readers that I just learned about Ken Carey in May, having just read Geoff Stray's book.[19] My sense is that a thorough reading of Carey's books would reveal many more parallels.

Maori Prophesy

While we're on the subject of Geoff Stray's work, it is interesting to note that the indigenous of New Zealand have their own prediction about 2012. Stray goes into an analysis of their linguistics before coming to the conclusion that their holy men see a "dissolving of the veil" in 2012, a "merging of the physical and spiritual planes."

If you remember what was communicated from the opening paragraph of Chapter 1 to the present text, you will note that this is yet another way of expressing what happens during the Passage.

Dr. Alexey Dmitriev
Dramatic Changes in Solar System Energetics

Dr. Dmitriev, an esteemed member of the Russian Academy of Sciences, has written extensively about changes in our solar system that Russian scientists have been observing since the 1960's. In connection with the "2012 phenomenon," Dmitriev has been written about by Spray, David Wilcock, Lawrence Joseph, and others. Without going into a detailed explanation of the physics, here's the short version:

As our solar system travels through space, there is a protective *heliosphere* that protects the sun and the objects within its sphere of influence from the negative effects of travelling through interstellar space. This heliosphere is comparable to the protective layers of the earth's

---

19   Stray, p. 40, 315.

atmosphere, but many times larger. In any event, the "shock wave" at the leading edge of the heliosphere — (think of your car's bumper) — has increased in size *1000%* since it was first observed and is continuing to expand rapidly. Dmitriev's conclusion? That our entire solar system is moving into a completely new energetic area.[20]

I add this as a nexus point because the kind of astrophysical event that has been described to me could hardly seem possible unless there were energetic conditions detectable throughout our solar system that were leading up to it ... for years. Dmitriev's research supports such a contention. Moreover, the astrophysical changes that have been occurring already are not nominal.

Synchronicities

They are dramatic.

Christine Breese, Ph.D.
Cuenca, Ecuador — May, 2012

Christine is a good friend of mine who lives here in Ecuador[21] and is currently completing the construction of her spiritual retreat.[22] In 1994 she went into a type of coma which some yogis refer to as a "spiritual sleep." Her sojourn lasted three days of earth time, but in "experiential time" amounted to a span she has estimated to be somewhere close to 40 years.

During her leave-of-absence, Christine was shown the unfoldment of an eschaton that bears remarkable similarity to the particulars revealed in my own ayahuasca sessions. Stated briefly, she saw pockets of communities forming all over the earth in response to the escalating evil and corruption which dominated world affairs. Mankind would divide into two camps: those who benefited from the mire, wanted things to continue as they were, or didn't care; and those who wanted to return to their spiritual roots. The development of the heart was central to not only joining a community but remaining in one. In fact, community members actively worked at "keeping up their vibration" to remain inside

---

20 *Stray*, p. 180-188.

21 Christine Breese is the founder of the University of Metaphysical Sciences (www.umsonline.org), which has tens of thousands of students all over the world who either take a few courses for personal enrichment or are in the process of earning their degrees. She has been a spiritual leader, healer, author, and teacher for the past twenty years. At this time, she is living in Ecuador at Gaia Sagrada (see next footnote), continuing to develop and facilitate spiritual courses and classes

22 Christine Breese is also the founder of Gaia Sagrada Spiritual Retreat Center (www.GaiaSagrada.com) in Ecuador. Located in the Andes Mountains outside Cuenca on 55 acres of pristine land, her center offers up to 150 courses and workshops within a spiritually focused, living community.

their community. As more and more like-minded souls congregated in the self-sufficient, spiritual communities, power-hungry interests — which have for eons been at the foundation of politics around the world — determined that these spiritual communities must be destroyed. Initially, infiltrators were sent to co-opt the communities. When these agents either disappeared, joined the communities and abandoned their allegiance to the dark forces, or otherwise failed to complete their mission, stronger measures were employed — eventually leading to military operations to have these spiritual centers bombed.

Christine saw the centers as spiritually protected by divine intervention such that even bombs dropped by military aircraft failed to touch them. She describes the centers as protected by "bubbles" — or impenetrable membranes, until what results is a SPLIT into two worlds, a spiritually-regenerated New Earth and an Old Earth. The vibrations of those at the spiritual centers becomes so incompatible with those of the rest of the world that they can no longer co-exist. Interestingly, she describes the New Earth as a heavenly paradise and the Old Earth as a living hell.

Christine doesn't deny that there are elements of what was shown to her that could be metaphorical or symbolic. (I would have to say the same about the information I have received.) Nor is she definitive about the time line; in fact, she was never shown one. Her sense, however, is that these developments are coming soon.

Synchronicity

The SPLIT into two earths bears remarkable resemblance to what I was shown. The qualitative description of these earths is nearly identical. The importance of "heart development" is a dominant theme in both Christine and my own visions.

Toni Toney — May, 2012

Toni is an author, lecturer, nutritionist, and a personal friend of 20 years.[23] Although I haven't seen Toni in person in more than ten years, we've kept in touch by phone. In mid-May we were able to compare notes via phone about our respective visions.

In 2007 Toni received a series of dramatic revelations about the future, the destiny of the Earth, and an end-time eschaton. Interestingly, she received these angelic communications while visiting the Greek island

---

23　Toni Toney is best known for her current work, *The Get Clean, Go Green Ecodiet*, available in health food stores throughout the U.S. and all major online bookstores. See (http://www.getcleangogreenecodiet.com)

of Patmos, meditating very near the place where St. John inscribed *The Book of Revelations* nearly 2,000 years earlier. In 2010 Toni returned to Patmos, where the visions continued and additional details were added.

To summarize, Toni was shown how man devolved away from God, "looking outside of ourselves and losing contact with the Divine within." The Earth became not simply a place to enjoy the many manifestations of God, but a source of exploitation. "Men saw a material world, not a physical world."

Like Christine and myself, Toni has been shown a Split into an Old and New Earth. "Spiritual regeneration requires it. You can't put new wine into an old wine vat." To hear Toni explain her visions is to feel that St. John has returned and is just picking up where he left off. The lexicon of expressions, the phraseology, is eerily familiar and there is a continuity with the earlier work. "Early on I was told not to worry about the melting of the polar ice cap, as this was the opening of the Earth's Seventh Seal."

Although a Split into an Old and New Earth — one hellish and the other heavenly — is shared in both of our visions, the process itself is communicated differently. Toni was shown the New Earth already growing within the current one, as if Mother Earth were pregnant. There is a hidden portal near the physical north pole that will expand — (it is already a point of egress for a civilization far more advanced than our own living deep within the earth, she says) — and from this orifice a New Earth will emerge.

Like Christine and myself, Toni doesn't attempt to parse the communications into which portions may be metaphorical. However, a Split, not only into a Old and New Earth but within humanity between those who are prepared and those who are not, is a relentless theme. So dominant has this theme appeared within her visions that she is now devoting her life to helping people prepare.

In order to send this book to press before the end of June, we are now closing with the above Nexus Points while continuing to expand on this work at www.Gospel2012.com. If you wish to read further or contribute to this discussion, we urge you to participate on our website today.

As we proceed together towards the Passage and you intensify your "personal search," you will find that you are not alone. You will find that there are opportunities to network with other awakening hearts that can feel the same call. Synchronicities will guide you when you least expect them. Then you will find that an image of the New Earth is emerging not because it was sitting there waiting for you to find it . . . rather, it came into existence with the Love and Grace of a Creator — the long lost lover you never knew about — who has waited billions of years to get you back.

And together you created it.

~ Greg Caton — (taken from Chapter 10, "Conclusion")

About the Author

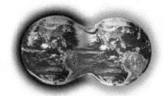

Greg Caton is a practicing herbalist and has authored three previous books – (see www.gregcaton.com). He founded Alpha Omega Labs in the early '90's, which specializes in researching time-tested, herbal compounds traditionally used to treat cancer – (see www.altcancer.net). His experiences in alternative medicine are detailed in the free, online book Meditopia® (www.meditopia.org), a work-in-progress.

He lives with his family and expat friends in Cuenca, Ecuador.